Devotion to Saint Ignatius

by Fr. Marin de Boylesve

Translated and Annotated by
E.A. Bucchianeri

Devotion to Saint Ignatius

by Fr. Marin de Boylesve, S.J.

Translated and Annotated by
E.A. Bucchianeri

Batalha Publishers
Fatima, Portugal ©2023

This new English edition has been translated and annotated by E.A. Bucchianeri ©2023 from the augmented Second Edition published by Jules Vic Library, Paris, 1880.

ISBN: 978-989-53726-4-5

Table of Contents

ଛ ❖ ଓ

APPENDIX

<u>About this Edition</u>

This has been translated from the augmented Second Edition published by Jules Vic Library, Paris, 1880, and features British spelling. New material in this edition includes the biography of the author, illustrations, the annotations, and the appendix.

E.A. Bucchianeri

<u>About the Author</u>

Fr. Marin de Boylesve was born on November 28, 1813 at the Château de la Coltrie in the commune of Saint-Lambert de la Potherie near Angers. He came from a distinguished aristocratic family whose name can be traced back many centuries as seen in Abbé Jean-Baptiste Ladvocat's *Dictionnaire historique portatif* (1755). Fr. Marin descended directly from Eslienne Boyliaue (or Boilyeve), the great statesman and the principal adviser of St. Louis IX, King of France. Other illustrious ancestors included intrepid knights, one in particular also named Marin joined the cause of King Henry IV. After the Battle of Arques, the king called him 'his beloved knight', granted him a heredity knighthood in 1597, then was made Seigneur de la Maurouziere in 1598 thereby granting him the right to add three gold fleur-de-lis to the top of his arms and bear the signs of the Order of St. Michel in his escutcheon. He was also appointed lieutenant-general of Anjou and councillor of state as a reward for his dedication. Another Marin Boylesve appears in the family line, the third to hold the name, and was in service to King Louis XIV as manager of his hôtel.

Loyal to the French King and to their Catholic faith, many members of the family were forced to emigrate during the French Revolution, but some members stayed behind in their beloved France. Fr. de Boylesve would recall a favourite family story, of how his grandmother was imprisoned in Angers by the Revolutionaries and managed a daring escape on the road during a prisoner transfer to the local castle. While she pretended to pick up a dropped package, a solider kicked her into the ditch. She took the opportunity to flee to a nearby house. However, when they threatened to imprison those harbouring escaped prisoners, she bravely marched straight in to the Revolutionary Office and gave herself up to ensure the safety of those who sheltered her. The revolutionaries did not dare risk upsetting the populace as her father was the former mayor of Angers before the Revolution and loved by the people. They decided to let her return to her father's house.

Fr. de Boylesve was the last direct descendant of his distinguished line, having followed the call to enter the Company of Jesus, or Jesuits, which also is a remarkable story of a predestined vocation. The Jesuits were persecuted due to fears they were growing in power and wealth. Pressured by the royal courts of Europe, Pope Clement XIV suppressed the Society, forcing members of the order to renounce their vows and go into exile. They were expelled from France in 1764. Fr. de Boylesve's mother, Clémentine de Livonnière, made a solemn promise on the day of her wedding that if God permitted the Jesuits to return to France and she was granted a son, she would offer him to the order and entrust him to it. As mentioned, Fr. Marin was born in 1813, a year before 1814 when Pope Pius VII restored the Society. Tragedy struck when Marin's father died, Marin was only ten months old at the time, but keeping her promise his mother dutifully sent him for his education at the age of ten to the Jesuit Fathers of Montmorillon. The moment he arrived at the school and saw a Jesuit for the first time who happened to be the Superior of the college Fr. Michel Le Blanc, he heard an inner voice say to him: "Little one, that is what you will be."

Fr. de Boylesve entered the school as a student and was destined never to leave the Jesuits. In 1831 he turned eighteen, a year after the July Revolution of 1830, which saw the rightful king to the French throne Charles X overthrown. His heir, Henry V the 'Miracle Child', was forced into exile at the age of ten, his throne usurped by the man who had been approached to be his regent, Louis-Philippe, Duke of Orléans. The events of the times burned the hearts of the faithful as the historical church of the royal family, Saint-Germain-l'Auxerrois, was profaned. Paris was sacked, and wayside devotional crosses and shrines over large areas of France were destroyed as Catholic legitimist symbols of Charles X, even those which had no royal significance or connection to the king.

Fr. Marin had just completed his schooling when he formally announced his decision to enter the Society, the historic events of the previous year and their aftermath no doubt influencing his decision.   Writing to his grandmother he declared:

"The course of my studies completed I could not remain without doing anything. God will ask us for an exact account of all the moments He gives us. Full of this thought I ardently wished to serve my country and the Church especially. At a time when both are in such great peril, as a Frenchman and as a Christian, I felt the need to throw myself into the thick of the fray. To take place in the first rows under the banners of religion whose triumph alone can bring glory and happiness back to my homeland, to serve immediately under my first head Jesus Christ, to be one of His companions, seemed to me the most glorious at the same time as most useful for my neighbour. Immense advantages, treasures of happiness and glory, the hundredfold from this life of all that I would give to the Lord, all of these promised in the gospel by Jesus Christ, strongly attracted me to be generous. What more could I do than give myself? (...)"

His family strongly opposed, especially as he was the last direct heir to the Boylesve house, but his mother let him go despite the great sacrifice, no doubt she understood God was accepting her promise to give him to the Jesuits, and not just for his education but now was asking for his whole life, a bitter dreg for her down to the last drop of the cup.

He entered the Novitiate in 1831 at Estavayer in the canton of Fribourg in

Switzerland with two other students. As they arrived at their new school, they rang the doorbell at the moment the house clock struck three. The Father who received them remarked: "You are entering at the hour of the Sacred Heart." This introduction to a new school would once again give Fr. de Boylesve a sign regarding the future work he would one day accomplish, although on this occasion he did not know it at the time. He made his first vows at the Maison du Passage on October 10, 1833. He studied philosophy and then in 1835 became a supervisor at the Collège de Mélan, a position he held for one year. He remained in the same college until 1842 where he was in succession professor of grammar, humanities and rhetoric. He thoroughly enjoyed his work with the students, writing in 1837:

"I find this job a lot of fun, despite the hardships that come with it. I have forty students; I love them and I try to spare nothing to make them good Christians, educated Christians capable of one day rendering true service to religion and to the state. It is the sight of such a noble ending that sustains and animates me." In the same letter he continues, regarding his concern for his family, "(...) the only important thing is, is everyone behaving well and does he remember the motto of the family, RELIGIO, PATRIA? For me who gave up everything, even my name which will be extinguished in my person, I remember it, and God grant that I am consumed and that I use myself in the service of one and of the other."

Although renouncing his aristocratic life he never gave up its noble spirit represented by the family motto, an ardent loyalty to the Catholic faith of his forefathers and his country. In the title pages of his texts he included the family crest of three crosses and motto: RELIGIO, PATRIE – "Faith and Country". Those who knew him and his 'military' style ways said he was just like the loyal intrepid knights of old.

At the end of 1842 he returned to France. He took theology courses at Laval for four years. Instinctively he was drawn to the writings of St. Thomas Aquinas and steered clear of new systems that deviated from the philosophical teachings of the Seraphic Doctor. In 1846 theology training completed, Fr. Boylesve was sent by his superiors to Angers, then in his third year at Notre-Dame d'Ay. In 1848 he was appointed to Brugelette, where he occupied the chair of philosophy. One student who fondly recalled Fr. de Boylesve and his time at Brugelette said his arrival was providential. His classes were easy to follow, his manner clear and crisp, but this is not all that gained the respect of the students. In 1848 they were restless as revolution was in the air, Louis-Philippe I, who had overthrown Catholic King Charles X was now in his own turn overthrown. Rising above and beyond what was required of his philosophy courses, Fr. Boylesve seized the opportunity like a knight-commander of old to direct the lazy students yet bursting with energy towards something constructive: Catholic action to fashion them into vigorous young men of service for Church and country. With his apostolic action he captivated the students with his literature classes, speaking on many subjects from philosophy, history, politics both ancient and modern. He particularly drew them with his catechism lessons on the Council of Trent, his clarity and enthusiasm captivating them.

As Fr. de Boylesve loved his students he was equally admired and loved by them, earning the nickname 'The Captain' as a mark of respect. The students composed a military style tune for his birthday, the refrain remaining popular and hummed everywhere: "Courageous Captain, lead us into battle." A student recalls: "I understood all that was apostolic about his action on us. We can sum it up by saying that he made it his mission to preach to us always and everywhere the contemplation of Saint Ignatius on the Reign of Jesus Christ as it is given in the *Exercises*." In 1851 Fr. Boylesve was sent to Vannes where he was made prefect of studies, his nickname 'The Captain' following him. In October 1853 he left the post and resumed teaching philosophy, a position that he would keep for a long time, either in Poitiers or in Vaugirard.

Known to be quiet and reserved when on his own, it was another matter when he was teaching or publicly speaking. He was incapable of remaining silent or softening his direct manner of expression when it was a question of truth, and did not hold back when it came to defend the Faith and the Church against unbelievers, becoming as noted like his knight-ancestor of old, charging forth to give chase and defeat any bold rascal on the field of battle albeit with his tongue and writings rather than with a literal sword. His attitude is quaintly summed up by the art critique he once gave of the statue of the fountain of St. Michael in Paris, complaining with slight annoyance that the mighty archangel was made to look too carefree and benevolent when dispatching Satan: "See then, it is that he seems to spare him!"

He was also a zealous worker and relished activity. He once wrote: "I challenge my superiors to give me too much work." In addition to his religious duties and teaching, he was a prolific writer, his output seeming to have no end. He wrote on a myriad of subjects and in different genres, from devotional booklets and pamphlets to history, literature, philosophy, Biblical dramas, summaries of the Church Fathers and Doctors, his own sermons, studies of the Scriptures, Our Lady, the *Spiritual Exercises* of St. Ignatius just to name a few, there were always more plans for further works in progress, his room filled with notes and notebooks. He was always studying as well, also making it a practise to read through the entire Bible every year. One might call him a workaholic in today's terms, but it was noted he believed in a time and a place for everything and diligently managed his hours. He enjoyed recreation time, especially going for walks, and did not sacrifice rest.

Despite his zest for work, he disapproved of a few young professors who sacrificed too much sleep and recreation time for their studies, endangering their health. Yet, while sparing of his time, he was ever charitable and ready to help another all for the glory of God.

In September 1870 Fr. de Boylesve was sent to the College of Le Mans, Notre-Dame de Sainte-Croix, when the Franco-Prussian war was raging and France suffered the indignity of invasion. The humiliation felt by the country also struck the pious and patriotic Fr. de Boylesve to the core: "I searched through the memories of my life; I do not remember ever having felt greater pain than this, not even when I learned of my mother's death. This humiliation of France, the Eldest Daughter of the Church, thus succumbing before Prussia, the Eldest Daughter of Protestantism, in the face of the whole world, is something unheard of."

The Messenger, the magazine of the Apostleship of Prayer run by the Jesuits, began spreading the visions of St. Margaret Mary, declaring the only way France would be saved from her enemies was to embrace the devotion to the Sacred Heart. The message inspired Fr. de Boylesve. He became a chaplain to the Catholic Papal Zouaves, forces sent to defend the French Motherland from the Protestant invaders, giving them rousing sermons: "Clotilde, inspiring faith in Clovis, saved the Franks and slaughtered the Germans at their feet ... Joan of Arc by her standard delivered France from the English!

Your standard is the Sacred Heart." The Zouaves placed the Sacred Heart on their banner. Fr. de Boylesve also busily spread Sacred Heart badges of wool for the soldiers to pin on their uniforms, for they were in high demand. A gifted and inspiring preacher, his sermons encouraged them onward, even when they were driven back in defeat by the Prussians to where the soldiers remarked: "This man can lead us to the fire tomorrow; we would gladly be killed for him."

Fr. de Boylesve is fondly remembered today in Catholic circles in France for his work as the director of the Apostleship of Prayer in Le Mans through which he contributed to the spread of devotion to the Sacred Heart. On October 17, 1870 Fr de Boylesve was appointed to preach at the Visitation of Le Mans upon St. Margaret Mary for his subject, who at the time was a Blessed. He also preached upon another mystic who had died within their own times, Mother Marie de Jesus (1797-1854) from the convent des Oiseaux of Paris who had received revelations from the Sacred Heart that were favourably recognised by the Archbishop of Paris. On June 21, 1823 the Sacred Heart revealed to Sr. Marie of Jesus that He desired France be consecrated to His Sacred Heart by the King, and that a chapel be built and dedicated to Him, and the feast of the national consecration be formally celebrated every year. "After my sermon," recounts Fr. Boylesve, "the Mother Superior expressed to me her astonishment at my silence with regard to an almost similar order that Our Lord had given to Blessed Margaret Mary on June 17th, 1689. I confessed that in our college, which had barely opened for a month, I had not found the letters of the Blessed One and that I was unaware of the apparition and the order she was telling me about. I promised to make good this omission." Apparently at that time, the Sacred Heart's requests to St. Margaret Mary for a shrine and the national consecration of France by the King were not yet widely known.

True to his word, filled with his characteristic zeal for faith and country, doing what he could to extend the reign of Jesus Christ through his beloved homeland and secure its safety, the very next day he repaired his omission by publishing a pamphlet featuring the prophecies of St. Margaret Mary and Mother Marie de Jesus entitled "Triumph of France by the Sacred Heart", composing a special prayer of consecration, which the Zouaves said every Friday as hope in the Sacred Heart was sorely needed. Paris was threatened with destruction by bombardments, then starvation by the invading Prussians, having commenced a siege around the city in September 1870. The siege continued until January 1871, the citizens reduced to dire circumstances. The zoo animals were slaughtered for food, the populace also living off of stray animals and rats. While the Prussian advance had ceased, humiliation still ensued when France suffered defeat at the hands of the Prussians with the establishment of the German Empire, also losing the territory of the

Alsace-Lorraine to the victors. The troubles were not over. From March to May 1871 Paris fell into the clutches of the anticlerical socialist Communards, rebels revolting against the new government of the Third Republic. Blood ran in the streets, historical buildings burned, including the Tuileries Palace. The anticlerical Communards also executed the Archbishop of Paris, Georges Darboy, fulfilling the prophecy of St. Catherine Laboure. This horrific turn of events, combined with the circulation of prophecies foretelling the destruction of Paris was at hand, the faithful no doubt felt doom hung over the city. The times were desperate. After several reprintings, including a full reproduction of the text by Fr. Ramiere in the 'Messenger' newsletter issued by the Apostleship of Prayer, more than 330,000 copies of Fr. de Boylesve's pamphlets of the 'Triumph of the Sacred Heart' were circulated. It contributed to the rapid spread devotion to the Sacred Heart and bolstered the call to have the Universal Church consecrated to the Sacred Heart, also to build a national shrine on Montmartre in atonement for the atrocities committed by the Communards who began their uprising there. Construction began in 1875, the cornerstone was laid on June 16, 1875, the day Bl. Pius IX encouraged all the faithful to pray the consecration to the Sacred Heart using the special formula composed by the Sacred Congregation of Rites for the 200th anniversary of the apparition of the Sacred Heart to St. Margaret Mary. The construction of Sacre

Coeur was at last completed in 1914.

As for Fr. Boylesve, in addition to his efforts to spread devotion to the Sacred Heart he worked unceasingly at many other endeavours, not only as director of the Apostolate of Prayer in Le Mans, but also with the Confraternities of Saint Joseph such as that of the Good Death, and also the Confraternity of the Agonizing Heart, the Work of Campaigns, Conferences of St. Vincent de Paul, Workers' Circles, he still appeared to dare all and sundry that they would never be able to find enough work for him to do. He amazed all that he was never at a loss for a subject to preach upon. He could easily vary his sermons to where it appeared he never preached the same way twice, and always captured his hearers' attention. One day out of curiosity a hardened sinner walked in to listen to him preach and left a converted man.

When Fr. Boylesve was not working, he was praying. There was no question that he maintained a deep spiritual life. He was transferred to Vaugirard in 1875, returning to Le Mans two years later in 1877. Three years later his teaching came to an end at the college there with the decree of March 29, 1880 issued by the French minister for public education prohibiting the Jesuits from engaging in their educational apostolate, only the first of several anticlerical laws that would be passed in France over the next decades. Fr. Boylesve admitted he was on the verge of tears saying his last Mass for the students in the chapel before the school closed.

Yet, he remained as active as ever despite this terrible blow, preaching, giving catechisms and continuing his writing, tackling the problems of the day threatening both the Church and society.

He continued working despite his old age, until the end of 1891 when his activity was curtailed. He was struck with various ailments, first a tormenting dermatitis that remained with him, then inflammation of the blood that restricted his activities for many weeks, although he managed to say Mass and continue his writing, until at last he was struck with paralysis, unable to walk or speak. Clutching his rosary and his crucifix, the ever zealous 'priest-knight' of the Vendée gave up his soul to God in February 22, 1892 and was buried in the Jesuit cemetery of Sainte-Croix.[1]

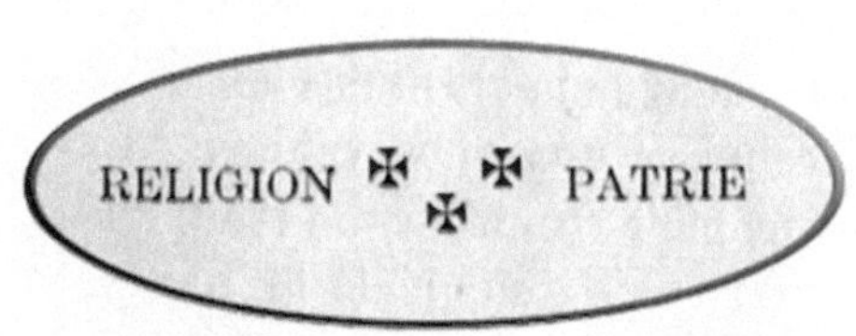

---

1   Biographical information from 'Necrologie. Le Père Marin de Boylesve, in 'Lettres de Jersey', Vol.XII, No. 1 (April 1893)

<u>Forward by the Author</u>

What we offer here is taken from various printed sheets without the name of the author, or, from the writings of St. Ignatius himself. The novena opens with a dramatised meditation, the features of which we have borrowed from sacred text. It would be easy to set to music the Latin words of this Oratorio. This collection ends with a canticle that we composed on a well-known tune, which is one of the most beautiful inspirations of Fr. Lambillotte.

Fr. Marin de Boylesve

St. Ignatius of Loyola

Abridgement of His Biography,
Taken from His Office

*(For a more detailed biography,
see the text written by Fr. Weninger In the Appendix)*

1: Ignatius, born at Loyola in Navarre, of an illustrious family of Spain, attached himself first to the court of the Catholic king, and then served in his armies. A wound he received at the siege of Pamplona caused him a dangerous illness, during which by chance[2] he read some books of piety, and this reading inspired him with the most ardent desire to walk in the footsteps of Jesus Christ and His saints. He went to Montserrat. After hanging his worldly armour before the altar of the Blessed Virgin, he spent the whole night in prayer, and thus tested the holy militia. He stripped himself of his precious clothes, put them on a poor man, then covered himself with sackcloth and left for Manresa. There for a year he gave himself up to pious rigours of mortification. His food was bread he begged for and water was his drink. He fasted every day except Sundays. He tamed his flesh by wearing a chain bristling with spikes and

---

2 That is, during the period of his recovery.

a coarse hair shirt. He had no other bed than the ground, and he scourged himself with an iron discipline until he bled. But God favoured him with revelations so luminous that he used to say the following: "Even if the Divine Scriptures did not exist, the extraordinary knowledge that the Lord gave me at Manresa would suffice to dispose me to die for the Faith." It was then that the man who had no inkling of the *belles-lettres*, composed the book of the *Spiritual Exercises*, an admirable work, the merit of which is proved by the approval of the Holy See and by the usefulness which all the world draws from it.

2:    But, to form himself better for the conquest of souls, he thought he should employ the aid of *belles-lettres*, and began to study grammar with the children. However, his zeal for the salvation of souls did not wane. Penalties, insults, outrages, imprisonments, almost mortal blows, nothing put him off. He endured everything with admirable patience, and he would have liked to suffer even more for the glory of his Master. While in Paris, he joined nine companions from different countries, all of whom were masters of arts and graduated in theology from the University of that city, and he laid the first foundations of his order in the church of Montmartre. He then established it in Rome, and he attached it to the Apostolic See by the closest knots, joining to the three ordinary vows a fourth vow relative to the missions. This order was first admitted and confirmed by Paul

III, he soon had the approval of the Popes his successors, and that of the Council of Trent.

St. Ignatius sent St. Francis Xavier to India to preach the Gospel there; he disseminated his other companions in different countries to propagate the faith there. He therefore declared war against pagan superstition and heresy, and this war was continued with the greatest success. It was also generally thought (and this feeling was supported by the authority of the Sovereign Pontiff) that God, who gives His Church defenders according to the times, had raised up St. Ignatius and the Society of which he was the founder, to oppose Luther and the other heretics of that century.

3: He was above all concerned with reviving piety among Catholics. The decoration of churches, the more assiduous teaching of the catechism, the practice of preaching, the frequenting of the sacraments, were the happy fruits of his care and solicitude. He opened classes everywhere to educate youth in literature and religion, established the Germanic College in Rome, erected monasteries for girls who had lost or were in danger of losing their innocence. He founded his communities for orphans and catechumens of both sexes. He did many other good works, and worked with untiring ardour to earn souls for God. Sometimes they heard him say: "If I were free to choose, I would rather go on living in the service of God and neighbour, with the uncertainty of enjoying heavenly goodness, than to die on the spot with the assurance of entering into eternal bliss."

He exercised an astonishing command over the demons. St. Philip Neri and others saw rays of Divine light shining on his face. Finally, at the age of sixty-five years he went to meet his Lord, whose greatest glory had always been the object of his talks and the motive of his actions. Gregory XV placed this illustrious man in the rank of saints, in whom the merit of having rendered great services to the Church was elevated by the brilliance of miracles.

St. Ignatius – A Dramatic Meditation

Based on the Bible

Luther: No, I will not serve.

The People: Come, let us break our chains, and shake off the yoke of Rome.

God: Who will I send? Who will march to support Our cause?

Narrator: And then there was a man, called Ignatius, a man of counsel and strength.

Satan: (*To Ignatius*): See these honours, I will give you all this, if you fall at my feet and worship me.

God: It was for My glory that I created him, for that I trained him, for that I made him. – I called you by your name, you are Mine.

Pleasure: (*Tempting Ignatius*), Come, let us enjoy the present goods; let us crown ourselves with roses before they fade.

God: For the victor I reserve a hidden manna.

Pride: (*Tempting Ignatius*), Come, let us raise a town and a tower, to immortalize our name.

God: Come, and I will make you the father of a whole people, and your name will be great.

Ignatius: Lord, what do you want me to do?

God: Go in the strength that I have given you and you will deliver Israel from the hand of Madian; know that it was I who sent you.

Heresy: No, I will not serve.

The People (*following Heresy*): Let us break our irons.

Ignatius: Yes, I will go against this giant who insults the people of God.

The Angels (*to Ignatius*): Come, and help us.

Ignatius: If there is anyone who still loves his God, join me.

Xavier and the other Companions of the Saint: We are yours, O my Father, we will walk with you, O Ignatius.

Ignatius: Go, ignite, ignite all hearts.

The Angels: How beautiful are the feet of those
who announce peace, who announce
the good news.

God: And they will announce My glory to the
nations, and they will bring all your brothers to
My holy mountain of Jerusalem.

Narrator: All rivers flow into the sea,
and the sea does not overflow.

Ignatius (*dying*) speaks to his Company: Ask
what you want of me before I'm taken from you.

The Company: My Father, my Father, give us
your double spirit.[3]

------

3   'Double spirit': i.e. a 'double portion of your spirit" -
the same request made by Eliseus to Elias before he
was taken to heaven in the fiery chariot. According to
the Douay-Rheims Bible 'double spirit' means: "A
double portion of thy spirit, as the eldest son and heir:
or thy spirit which is double in comparison of that
which God usually imparteth to his prophets."
Therefore, Eliseus was asking to be considered like an
eldest son and his spiritual heir as prophet and that he
may receive the greater portion of his prophetic spirit.
Fr de Boylesve is recreating this in his mini-drama, the
Jesuits in the Company of Jesus ask St. Ignatius before
his death for a greater portion of his great zeal and
spirit for the conversion of souls for the glory of God.

NOVENA

(Note: Considering Fr de Boylesve gives minimal prompts to reflect on, it might prove helpful to refer to the biography of St. Ignatius by Fr. Weninger in the Appendix while meditating upon these various points during the Novena.)

Vigil of the Novena

The demon prepares Luther in the cloister, and God prepares St. Ignatius in the camps.[4]

---

4   Apparently, Fr de Boylesve suggests that on the vigil, that is, on the day before making the novena, that we reflect and make the following meditation on how God works to thwart the devil. While Satan was forming the educated Luther, even in a cloister, turning the monk away from the path of holiness and moulding him into his evil tool to strip souls away from God and the Faith, God in turn took a proud and vain soldier bent on attaining worldly honours from out of the vulgar army camps and raised him up to work for His glory by having him found a new order in the Church and thereby battle against the evil caused by Luther.

First Day (Three Thoughts)

1: St. Ignatius, a military man. This is a preparatory career for the purposes of God. *Militia is vita hominis*: ("The life of man upon earth is a warfare," Job 7:1) *Labora ut bonus miles Christi Jesu:* ("Work like a good soldier of Jesus Christ" - 2 Tim. 2:3). *Apud Deum*, said St. Chrysostom, *militat etiam femineus sexus*; ("In God's eyes even women fight, "[5])

---

[5]   For context, Fr de Boylesve is noting the spiritual battle is not reserved just for men, women too are called to battle. This line is from St. Chrysostom, quoted by St. Thomas Aquinas in his answer regarding the question if the sacrament of Confirmation should be given to all. Since it is a sacrament which strengthens the Christian for spiritual battle, he argued that women should indeed be given the sacrament, for quoting St. Chrysostom: "(*Hom. i De Machab.*), *in earthly contests fitness of age, physique and rank are required; and consequently slaves, women, old men, and boys are debarred from taking part therein. But in the heavenly combats, the Stadium is open equally to all, to every age, and to either sex.* Again, he (St. Chrysostom) says (*Hom. de Militia Spirit.*): <u>*In God's eyes even women fight,*</u> *for many a woman has waged the spiritual warfare with the courage of a man. For some have rivaled men in the courage with which they have suffered martyrdom; and some indeed have shown themselves stronger than men.* Therefore this sacrament should be given to women." (St. Thomas Aquinas, 'Summa Theologiae - III', Q. 72, A. 8).

2:   He is injured in Pamplona.   Happy injury! *Glorificetur Filius Dei ex ed;* ("the Son of God will be glorified." John 11:4)[6]

3:   He is converted: First, in his bed; Second, while reading the Lives of the Saints. *Pauci ex infirmitate meliorantur:* ("there are few that illness makes better." Imitation of Christ. Kempis.)[7] For him the infirmary is salutary; he comes from it a different person.

<u>A Thought from St. Ignatius:</u>

"He who fears men too much, will do nothing great for God."

---

6   "And Jesus hearing it, said to them: This sickness is not unto death, but for the glory of God: that the Son of God may be glorified by it."   - (John 11:4)   Here we are to reflect on how God used St. Ignatius' injury, which seemed a misfortune, but became a blessed event that would change his life.

7   Basically, Kempis' line implies illness seems to bring out vices in the patient: i.e. such as impatience, etc. And, perhaps even grumbling against God, Who is usually unjustly blamed for the misfortune of illness. Here in contrast, Fr de Boylesve is showing the good example of St. Ignatius who proves the contrary. His illness became his means of conversion. Illness can be used to gain merits and make one holy if accepted properly and thereby the suffering is not wasted.

Second Day

1: The vigil of arms at Montserrat, the night before the Annunciation. *O beata nox!* O blessed night![8]

2: At Manresa he fasts, prays and is tempted as Our Lord was in the desert. This is he ordinary preparation for the apostolic life.

3: In Manresa, he writes the *Spiritual Exercises.* It is the book of the Christian soldier.

A Thought from St. Ignatius:

"We learned more in Manresa in a single hour under the guidance of God, than in all the books of the doctors."

---

8   St. Ignatius gave up his old sword to take on the arms of his new Master. As a true knight of Christ, he made an all night vigil as the knights of old who would make a night 'vigil of arms'.

St. Ignatius of Loyola in the Cave of Manresa

<u>Third Day (Three Thoughts)</u>

1: His pilgrimage to the Holy Land. Let us follow him in spirit and with him draw on the footsteps of Jesus the spirit of his true companions.[9]

---

9   His initial plan was to offer his life to God by staying in the Holy Land and literally follow in the footsteps of Christ for the salvation of souls. Six companions went with him. They started on this pilgrimage to the Holy Land, February 1523. They sailed from Barcelona to Gaeta, then went to Rome for Passion Week, and onward to Venice, where they sailed for Salamis, then to Joppa, arriving in Jerusalem in September. They had numerous adventures, threats of plague, dangers from criminals, sometimes he nearly starved, or perished from cold; ships on which they had been refused passage were wrecked. There were hardships of every sort. However, the Franciscans ordered them to return home. At first, St. Ignatius refused as he did not feel any danger, but the Franciscans explained they had orders from the Pope giving them authority to send pilgrims home for their own safety if necessary as Christians were known to get kidnapped and held for ransom, which caused their order many problems. They were about to show the official documents giving them this authority, and, explained disobedience to the rule was punishable by excommunication, but St. Ignatius declined to see them – if Rome had spoken, they would obey. St. Ignatius and his companions returned to Spain, although wondering what he was supposed to do as his plans were brought to nothing. But, as we know, God had other things in store.

2: He started studying when he was thirty-three years old. Never say: 'it is too late'.[10]

3:    He works for the salvation of souls among his fellow students. He is put in jail.[11]

A Thought from St. Ignatius:

"Do not undertake any business without consulting God in prayer."

---

10   Ignorant of Latin, he went to the grammar school for children in Barcelona to learn the language in order to be admitted to the University. Never say it is too late to start afresh! Begin from the bottom up if you have to. The important thing is, do not delay in doing what you know you have to do, even if it means starting from the ground up. Little by little wins the day, and progress is made. Blessed is he whom the Master finds doing what he is supposed to be doing.

11   After two years of study at the grammar school, he moved on to the University of Alcala. His zeal for the salvation of souls got him in trouble, for he would gather both students and adults to explain the Gospels and teach them how to pray. He attracted the attention of the Inquisition and he was thrown into jail, as anyone who was not ordained and caught teaching was considered suspect. When he was released, he was told to avoid teaching others. After this, he went to the University of Salamanca. Within two weeks of his arrival, he fell into the same trouble, the Dominicans had thrown him into prison again. Although they could find no heresy in what he taught, he was ordered to teach only children and then restrict his instructions to simple religious truths. This was not enough for him. Once more he took to the road, and this time he went to Paris.

Fourth Day

1: At the College of St. Barbe he resumed his studies. An impatient zeal does not push him to content himself with superficial or incomplete studies. He gives the example before imposing the precept.

2: He still works for the salvation of his fellow disciples. He wins St. Francis Xavier. How many souls are won in that one alone!

3: The first vows (of the Jesuit Order) are taken at Montmartre, the day of the Assumption. Let us undertake nothing without the help of Mary.

A Thought from St. Ignatius:

"Don't put off until tomorrow
what you can do today."

❖

<u>Fifth Day</u>

1: He is obliged to return to his country, he teaches the catechism to little children.

2: His life in the hospitals. The charity characteristic of his disciples for the hospitals. *Usque in praesentem diem.* (Until this day.) The Hôtel-Dieu is the hotel for the poor and the first hotel in a city.

3: Industrious charity to win souls. "Enter through their door," he said, "and lead them out through ours."

<u>A Thought from St. Ignatius</u>

"He who forgets himself for the service of God, can be assured that God will not forget him."

❖

<u>Sixth Day</u>

1: Motto of the Saint; *Ad majorem Dei gloriam.* (For the greater glory of God).[12] Let us renounce our own glory, if we want to procure that of God.

2: St. Ignatius wants his disciples, under the exterior of a common life, to be hidden in spirit and in a strongly tempered heart. *Magna facere* and *pati fortia*: great in action, strong in suffering.

3: Despite his character and his ardent zeal, the Saint wants us (i.e. members of the Order) to employ years in training and moulding the men of his Company.[13]

---

12   The motto of the Jesuits. The full phrase attributed to St. Ignatius is *Ad maiorem Dei gloriam inque hominum salutem* or "for the greater glory of God and the salvation of humanity." The motto is a reminder that any work as long as it is not evil, even if it would normally be considered inconsequential to the spiritual life, can be spiritually meritorious if it is performed in order to give glory to God.

13   I.e. the ardent zeal for the salvation of souls should not rush the spiritual formation of those joining the Jesuits. Imprudent haste can destroy spiritual formation.

"It is not enough to do good, it must be done well."

("A precious crown is reserved in heaven for those who put into their actions all the diligence of which they are capable, for it is not enough to do good, we must do it well.")[14]

Seventh Day

1: Obedience, the characteristic virtue of the Company of Jesus. It is that of the soldier, from the meticulous details of manoeuvre and discipline to the sacrifice of one's life. *Obediens usque ad mortem.* ("Obedient unto death.")[15] Without saying anything![16]

---

14   Note: this full quotation was not in the original text, it has been added to give further context regarding what St. Ignatius meant.

15   "He humbled himself, becoming obedient unto death, even to the death of the cross." (Philippians 2:8)

16   "He was offered because it was his own will, and he opened not his mouth: he shall be led as a sheep to the slaughter, and shall be dumb as a lamb before his shearer, and he shall not open his mouth." (Isaiah 53:7)

2: Le Jay, Laynes, and Salmeron are sent by the Pope to the Council of Trent, and by Ignatius to the hospitals and the poor of that city. *Ima summis jungere jesuiticum est.*[17] Humble yourself when God lifts you up.

3: Education of the youth, the first work of the Company of Jesus. Everything must be regulated in those who are the living ruler of others.[18]

<u>A Thought from St. Ignatius:</u>

"It is easier to listen than to speak.
Listen much, and talk little."

---

17   My rough translation, 'To join the Jesuits is to be the least and the great.' Or, the 'lowest and the highest'.

18   i.e. one must give good example as a superior and as a teacher first. St. Ignatius taught if you wish to convert another begin be reforming yourself first.

<u>Eighth Day</u>

1: Foreign missions, the second work. To support and encourage the Work of the Propagation of the Faith everywhere. It is a mass uprising, a spiritual crusade.

2: To give the *Spiritual Exercises*, third work. Make it your special study. *Timeo hominem unius libri*: "I fear the man of one book."[19]

3: To form and govern congregations of the Blessed Virgin. They are the soul of one college and one city.

---

19   A quote attributed to St. Thomas Aquinas, 'I fear the man of a single book'. Today, the meaning of the phrase has been twisted out of context to mean that someone 'fears' a person who is not widely read and educated because they fear the damage they could cause by their ignorance, but that is not what was meant. The original meaning is that one should 'fear' the formidable intellectual opponent who has dedicated himself to and become a master in a single chosen discipline rather than a 'jack of all trades' and master of none. Basically, a man who has thoroughly mastered the contents of one good book can be formidable. Fr de Boylesve says one can be a formidable master of the Catholic spiritual life and a stout enemy of error if you master this one good book given by St. Ignatius, the *Spiritual Exercises*.

A Thought from St. Ignatius

"There are few who understand what God could do with them, if only they gave themselves up entirely to His guidance."

Ninth Day

1: Consider that St. Ignatius made rules regarding modesty. Read them and take them to mind.

2: There is not an office which does not have its own rules, read those of your office and meditate on them. Order results from this individual punctuality (to the rules).[20]

3: Vow of profession: never to allow anything to be changed regarding poverty, except to restrict it further. Jesus Christ was not only addressing religious people when he said: 'Blessed are the voluntary poor'.[21]

---

20 For those who are not religious bound to a Rule, the laity can practice more diligence regarding their daily duties.

21 I.e. 'And every one that hath left house, or brethren,

<u>A Thought from St. Ignatius.</u>

Nothing is more dangerous in the divine service than negligence.

<u>Tenth Day: On the Feast Day – (Conclusion of the Novena)</u>

1: The principle and foundation (of the Jesuits): the glory of God.

2: The Reign of Jesus Christ: to know Jesus Christ, to love Him, to follow Him.

3: The two standards: Lucifer offers riches and honours; Jesus presents His cross, *there* is my standard.[22]

---

or sisters, or father, or mother, or wife, or children, or lands for my name's sake, shall receive an hundredfold, and shall possess life everlasting. And many that are first, shall be last: and the last shall be first. " (Matt. 19: 29-30)

22   I.e. Drawn from one of his more famous spiritual exercises.   Imagine a field of battle: on one side is Satan and his devilish army tempting you to join them under their banner, they are tempting you with all the pleasure this world has to offer. We know where that will lead in the end! Imagine Christ and His army of

4: The love of God: works more than words.

A Thought from Ignatius:

"There is no good in this life except what leads us to eternal life; there is no evil except what distracts from it, (I.e. distracts us from working towards eternal life). Adversities detach us from this world and bind us to the cross of Jesus Christ. If in this life we are crucified with Jesus, in the next we will be raised up with Him."

saints and angels on the other side, and the promise of everlasting bliss if you reject the passing pomps of this world and accept the Cross with its temporary sufferings and trials. Which banner attracts you? In whose army will you choose to fight?

AD   DEI
MAIOREM GLORIAM

<u>Prayer to St. Ignatius by Fr. Ribadeneyra</u>

<u>Translated and Arranged
in the Form of a Novena</u>[23]

Day 1:   O my tender father, holy priest, illustrious confessor, intrepid captain, faithful minister of God and glorious patriarch of so numerous a family! O most lovable Ignatius, glory of our age, ornament of religion, shield and bulwark of the Catholic Church which you have extended by yourself and by your children, and which you do not cease to extend and defend! O my father, you whom my soul venerates among all the friends and the elect of God with special respect and love, you in whom, after the most Blessed Virgin, Mother of God, and after my Guardian Angel, I have put all my hope in particular, I have recourse to you I address to you the cries of my heart and, prostrate at your feet, I humbly implore your favour and your help from the depths of this valley of tears and from the abyss of my sins and my miseries.

---

23   You can say the prayer in its entirety, or, section it into a novena as displayed.

Day 2: Holy saint, turn the eyes of your tenderness on the soul of this sinner that you see at your feet. Very gentle father, look kindly on your useless and imperfect son! You have already reached the port where you are safe, remember those who sail still exposed to a thousand dangers on this stormy sea. You have already obtained the palm of victory, help your soldiers who are exposed to all the traits of the enemy and who are surrounded on all sides.

Day 3: By that ineffable grace of which God predestined you, when being as if plunged into the abyss of the vanities of the world He called you and changed you into an entirely new man, confirming you and choosing you to render you glorious in heaven and on earth, I entreat you earnestly to obtain for me the forgiveness of the so numerous and serious sins by which I have offended the Divine Majesty before choosing you for my father and for my master, before having been enlightened by the ray of the divine vocation, before having received the celestial light which made me know and hate the miserable state of my soul.

Day 4: By that marvellous and divine spirit with which the Lord filled and imbued you to enable you to tolerate with invincible fortitude all the blows of poverty, deprivation, penance and austerity, all assaults of persecutions, anguishes, labours, dangers, sufferings, injuries and affronts

 which during all the time of your life you have gloriously endured for the love of Him, I beg you to intervene with your merits, in order May the Lord, who made you emerge victorious from all trials, forgive me all the faults I have committed out of sensuality and weakness, and so that from this day forward my soul may rise above this earth where I landed sadly dejected, and that animated by a divine force, I may imitate you and attach myself to your footsteps.

Day 5: By that light and the divine wisdom with which the Lord enlightened and adorned your soul by suggesting to you the idea of the order which you have founded, and inspiring you with the Rule of such a holy Institute and way of life, so perfect, so complete in all its parts, so proportioned to human weakness and so opportune in these unhappy times, I humbly beseech you O my tender father, to procure for me and for all your present and future sons from the Father of lights, Source of all good, from Whom you yourself have received this superior light, a grace that enlightens our souls and helps us to penetrate and know the excellence of this admirable Institute, so that, by knowing, loving and esteeming Him as He deserves, we would be resolved to spare no effort to vindicate this gift which we have received from the liberal and magnificent hand of the Lord Himself.

Day 6: By this infinite love and by this tender piety which led the Lord to make you father of so many sons, and founder of the little Company, and to propagate it throughout the earth by means of your double spirit of prudence and of magnanimity, so that everywhere we see your sons opposing the efforts of heresy, enlightening the infidels with the lights of faith, restoring among Catholics the practice of all the virtues and finally, reaping those abundant fruits which to our great joy they produce throughout the world, I beg you to obtain for us that the same Lord deign to continue and complete the work begun by the sovereign virtue of His right hand, that He resurrect and renew in your sons the inflamed zeal of the father, that He clothes us all with the spirit of poverty, may He corroborate us with contempt for the world and for ourselves, may He fortify us with a vigorous and ardent charity which makes us conquer for the love of Him all the difficulties that our glorious enterprise can offer.

Day 7: Obtain for us a deep inclination and a lively affection for continual and fervent prayer; a severe and careful mortification of our passions; a manner of acting which among ourselves is affectionate, peaceful and cordial, and which with strangers is modest, circumspect, grave, religious and agreeable; an angelic purity and chastity, an insatiable thirst to gain souls for God, an ardent desire to endure labours, persecutions and

injuries for their salvation; an indelible patience, an amiable gentleness, and final perseverance. In short, obtain for us your spirit and a grace so universal and so perfect that if it does not equal yours, at least let it approach that which you have received from the Lord for yourself and for us.

Day 8:   Give to the superiors a truly fatherly and godly spirit; to inferiors the spirit of obedience; to the masters of wisdom and to the disciples – humility, to the preachers a discreet zeal, to the confessors a efficacious compassion which helps them heal the wounds of sinners; to those who work for the conversion of heretics, faith and constancy; to those who, ablaze with the love of God, after having left their country and all the pleasures and comforts of life to carry the light of the Gospel to the blind, go to travel new worlds without being frightened from the diversity of climates nor from the distance of countries, to these heroes of charity obtain for them the apostolic spirit and an invincible force of soul; to our novices a perfect knowledge and great esteem for such a holy vocation; and to coadjutors devotion and humility; and above all, obtain for all of us that pure and right intention which makes us always seek in all our actions the greatest glory of God, as you yourself have constantly sought and procured it, wanting it to be the point of single target, the root, the essence and the foundation of your Institute.

9: O holy father! O blessed father! Communicate to your sons a portion of your spirit; however small that portion may be, it will suffice for all, and however multiplied the division you will make of it between us, you will not lose any of this spirit, but you will keep it whole and without any diminution, as Moses kept his after having divided it among the seventy-two elders. Grant us all that we ask of you; for although we recognize the Lord as the Author of all gifts and the Source from which emanates all that is good and perfect in heaven and on earth, you are so near to this Source of Life, you are so pleasing in the eyes of God, that it is impossible for us to doubt that you will obtain for us all that you ask for the good and for the perfection of the sons given to you by Him Who lives and reigns forever and ever. Amen.

Prayer to St. Ignatius
Translated from the Spanish[24]

Most holy father and patriarch, blessed Ignatius, whom Jesus gave as captain to His Company and whom He adorned with all the virtues that this high office requires:

Angel, by your purity of body and soul;

Archangel, by the high missions with which you have been charged for the honour of God and for the good of souls;

Principality, through the excellence of the direction that you have imprinted on thousands of persons;

Power, for the gift you received to cast out demons from bodies and souls,

Virtue, through the miracles without number that you have operated in favour of the those who have recourse to thee;

Domination, through the formation of the Company that you have hast instituted to make Jesus reign in all hearts;

Throne, for your zeal to expand the glory of God in all parts of the world;

Cherubim, through the lights which were communicated to you when you were writing the book of the *Spiritual Exercises* and the Constitutions of your Company;

---

24   The virtues of St. Ignatius are listed in comparison with those given to an angel in each of the Nine Choirs, from lowest to highest.

Seraph, by the fire which consumed you throughout your life and which inspired in you the desire to kindle in all souls the fire of the Divine Love;

A smaller version of paradise of numberless graces and virtues whose assemblage forms the incomparable heroism of your great soul. Thy child, O most loving father, pressed with the desire to love you and to make you loved, rejoices however to see you superior to all the praises his tongue can stammer and his understanding can conceive.

Full of confidence in your charity and in abandonment to your paternal goodness, I beseech you to obtain for me a truly holy life through the perfect observation of the commandments of God and of the evangelical counsels, and by the constant resolution not to seek anything in all my actions other than the greater glory of God.

Finally, may this life be crowned with a pleasing death before your eyes and in the arms of Jesus and Mary.

Yes I hope, O tender and beloved father, that you will obtain for me these favours so important for my salvation, and in particular the one that I ask of you by this novena, *(here name the special grace you desire or your request)*, for the greater glory of God, for your honour and for the spiritual advancement of my soul. Amen.

ഇ ❖ ൬

The Miracles of St. Ignatius

Litany in Honour of St. Ignatius

In Latin:

Kyrie eleison.
Christe eleison
Kyrie eleison.
Christe, *audi nos.*
Christe, *exaudi nos.*
Pater de coelis Deus, *miserere nobis.*
Fili, Redemptor mundi, Deus, *miserere nobis.*
Spiritus Sancte Deus, *miserere nobis.*
Sancta Trinitas, unus Deus, *miserere nobis.*
Sancta Maria, sine peccato origininali concepta,
    ora pro nobis.
Sancte Ignati, fundator Societatis Jesus,
    ora pro nobis. (etc.)
Beatae Virginis Mariae cultor addictissime,
Destructor haereseon,
Militantis Eccesiae subsidium,
Sacramentorum restaurator,
Pugnantium commilitonum robur,
Juventutis praesidium,
Vas electionis ut portet nomen Jesu,
Defensor religionis catholicae,
Vitiorum profligator,
Evangelicae veritatis propagator,
Majoris gloriae Dei praeco studiosissime,
Templum pacis et veritatis,
Christi laborum imitator,
Lumen et splendor orbis christiani,

Animarum moderator prudentissime,
Vitae spiritualis magister,
Spiritualium auctor Exercitiorum,
Condonator injuriarum,
Actuum et cogitationum exactor acerrime,
Speculum verae pietatis,
Humilitatis prodigium,
Aegrotantium salutis restitutor,
Mortuorum vita,
Miraculorum patrator,
Vestigator animarum,
Miserorum refugium,
Moerentium solatium,
Divini amoris incendium,
Obedientiae antesignane,
Castitatis amore et protectione admirabilis,
Paupertatis amantissime,
Salutis animarum zelator ardentissime,
Flagellum daemonum,
Omnium virtutum exemplar,
Divinis illustrationibus clarissime,
Mysterri SS. Trinitatis scrutator sanctissime,
Cultor specialis Angelorum,
Sollicitudine animarum Apostole,
Gratia et spiritu Propheta,
Austeritate vitae Martyr,

Agnus Dei qui tollis peccata mundi,
parce nobis Domine.
Agnus Dei qui tollis peccata mundi,
exaudi nos Domine.
Agnus Dei qui tollis peccata mundi,
miserere nobis.

V. Ora pro nobis, sancte Ignati,
R. Ut digni efficiamur promissionibus Christi.

Oremus: Deus, qui ad majorem nominis tui gloriam propagandam, novo per beatum Ignatium subsidio militantem Ecclesiam roborasti; concede ut ejus auxilio et imitatione certantes in terris, coronari cum ipso mereamur in coelis. Per Christum Dominum nostrum. Amen.

Translation:

Lord, *have mercy.*
Christ, *have mercy,*
Lord, *have mercy.*

Christ, *hear us.*
Christ, *graciously hear us.*

God the Father of Heaven, *have mercy on us.*
God the Son, Redeemer of the world,
    have mercy on us.
God the Holy Ghost, *have mercy on us.*
Holy Trinity, One God, *have mercy on us.*
Holy Mary, conceived without original sin,
    pray for us.
Saint Ignatius, founder of the Society of Jesus,
    pray for us. (etc.)
Dedicated devotee of the Blessed Virgin Mary,

Destroyer of heresy,
Support of the Church Militant,
Restorer of the sacraments,
The strength of fighting comrades,
Protector of youth,
Chosen vessel to uphold the name of Jesus
Defender of the Catholic religion,
Healer of vices,
Propagator of evangelical truth,
Most zealous herald of the greater glory of God,
Temple of peace and truth,
Imitator of Christ's labours,
Light and splendour of the Christian world,
Most prudent ruler of souls,
Teacher of the spiritual life,
Author of the Spiritual Exercises,
Pardoner of injuries,
Perceptive director of actions and thoughts,
Mirror of true piety,
Prodigy of humility,
Restorer of health to the sick,
Life for the dying,
Miracle worker,
Seeker of souls,
Refuge of the poor,
Comfort of the bereaved,
Fire of Divine love,
Sign of obedience,
Admirable in thy love and protection of chastity,
Most loving of poverty,
Zealous for the salvation of souls,
Scourge of demons,
Model of all virtues,

Clearly favoured by divine illuminations,
Most holy investigator of the mystery of the Most
Holy Trinity,
Special devotee of the Angels,
Apostle of concern for souls,
Filled with the prophetic grace and spirit,
Filed with the austerity of the martyr's life,

> Lamb of God, Who takest away the sins of
the world,
> > *Spare us, O Lord*
> Lamb of God, Who takest away the sins of
the world,
> > *Graciously hear us, O Lord*
> Lamb of God, Who takes away the sins of
the world,
> > *Have mercy on us*

> V. Pray for us, St. Ignatius,
> R. That we may be made worthy of the
promises of Christ

> *Let us pray:* God, Who for the greater propagation of the glory of Thy name, hath strengthened the militant Church Militant anew with the assistance of blessed Ignatius; grant that with his help in our struggles and by imitating him on earth, we may deserve to be crowned with him in heaven. Through Christ our Lord. Amen.

ℰ ❖ ℬ

Prayers by St. Ignatius

Suscipe (Take, Lord, Receive)

Take, Lord, receive all my liberty, my memory, my understanding, my whole will, all that I have and all that I possess. You gave it all to me, Lord; I give it all back to you. Do with it as you will, according to your good pleasure. Give me your love and your grace; for with this I have all that I need. Amen.

No Reward but to Do Thy Will - (Prayer of Generosity)

Dearest Lord, teach me to be generous; teach me to serve Thee as Thou dost deserve; to give and not to count the cost, to fight and not to heed the wounds, to toil and not to seek for rest, to labour and not to ask for reward save that of knowing I am doing Thy Will. Amen

Prayer to Jesus Crucified

O good Jesus! Most lovable Jesus, Who are the consolation, the strength and the hope of all those who call upon Your holy Name, and who take refuge in your salutary wounds, be with me Jesus through life and at death. Amen.

ဆ ❖ ၃

Prayer by St. Francis Xavier to St. Ignatius

O father of my soul, worthy of my deepest veneration, prostrate at your feet as if I saw you present, I humbly beg you to intercede for me without ceasing with God, so that He may give me the grace to know clearly and to perfectly fulfil His most holy Will. Amen.

ဆ ❖ ၃

St. Ignatius and St. Francis Xavier

Prayer to St. Ignatius

Latin: Ad. S. P. Ignatium:

O.B.P. Ignati, qui post Christum primus ac praecipuus fundator esse meruisti minimae Societatis Jesus, humiliter te precamur, ut tuâ omniumque filiorum tuorum, qui unà tecum jam praesenti Domini nostri aspectu fruuntur intercessione, nobis miseris licet et indignis peccatoribus, attamen sic quoque filiis tuis, impetres à Domino gratiam quâ omnibus diebus vitae nostrae ambulemus dignè vocatione nostra, in vera fide, spe firma, caritate ardenti, humilitate profunda, patientia perfecta, obedientia prompta, castitate pura, et altissima spiritus paupertate; ut ita in nobis et per nos planè impleatur ejus voluntas in vita et in morte, in tribulationibus et consolationibus, in labore et requie, secundum beneplacitum divinae ejus Majestatis. Amen.

O blessed father Ignatius, who through Christ merited to be the first and foremost founder of the smallest Society of Jesus, we humbly beseech you, that you, and all your children who have already gone together with you into in the presence of Our Lord and enjoy the honour of interceding, while we are poor and unworthy sinners, yet even so your children, may you obtain for us from the Lord the grace that during all the days of our lives we may proceed worthily in our vocation, in true faith, firm hope, burning love, profound humility, perfect patience, and prompt obedience pure chastity, and the most profound poverty of the spirit; so that in us and through us His Will may be fully fulfilled in life and in death, in tribulations and consolations, in labour and rest, according to the good pleasure of His Divine Majesty. Amen.

The Ten Sundays Devotion
In Honour of St. Ignatius of Loyola

In 1767, the Reverend Father Lorenzo Ricci, eighteenth general of the Company of Jesus, wanting to extend even further the devotion to St. Ignatius, had ten Sundays in honour of the holy Founder celebrated in the church of the Gèsu in Rome. He begged Pope Clement XIII to authorize this devotion and to grant indulgences to those who practised it.

It is not without reason that this devotion had been fixed on Sundays. This day is particularly consecrated by the Church to the devotion of the Most Holy Trinity. We know that St. Ignatius honoured with special affection this adorable mystery after the sublime knowledge of which that God had designed to grant him at the commencement of his conversion at Manresa. Besides, Sunday is the day of the week which should be used to glorify the Lord, and we also know that the motto of St. Ignatius was: 'For the greater glory of God.'. (For the number ten): the ten months the Saint spent in solitude at Manresa, where he composed his book of the *Spiritual Exercises,* and the ten years during which he governed his Company alone. And he had his *Constitutions* divided into ten parts, are worthy of singular attention. It is to honour his memory that they took the number of ten Sundays.

The Sovereign Pontiff (January 27, 1767), accorded a plenary indulgence for each of the ten consecutive Sundays immediately preceding the feast of St. Ignatius (July 31), or for each of the ten consecutive Sundays taken at any other time of the year, to all the faithful who, contrite, confess and receive Holy Communion, will sanctify these said days by pious meditations, prayers or other works of piety to the glory of God and in honour of the Saint, and will devoutly visit some church of the Company of Jesus. (Jesuits).[25]

⅚❖⅛

---

25 This Indulgence is listed in the Raccolta, which states: "The faithful who, on any of the ten Sundays preceding the Feast of St. Ignatius Loyola, or on any of the ten consecutive Sundays that they may choose during the year, spend some time in devout meditations or prayers in honour of the Saint, or who perform some other acts of devotion, are granted a plenary indulgence on the usual conditions. (S.C. Ind., Jan. 27, and Dec. 10, 1841). The Raccolta does not mention having to visit a Jesuit church or chapel, while the decree issued by the Congregation of Indulgences does mention the requirement Pent to visit a Jesuit church or chapel.

The Holy Water of St. Ignatius

Always admirable in His saints, the Lord, Who delights in manifesting the favour which they enjoy with Him, has distinguished among all, in these last centuries, St. Ignatius of Loyola, founder of the Company of Jesus. The Acts alone which were produced for the canonization of this man of God, legally recognized as many as two hundred miracles obtained through his intercession; also, the 19th of March, 1622, in bestowing the glorious title of saint to Ignatius, whose life had been consecrated to the most greater glory of God, the Church proclaimed illustrious not less by his miracles than by the heroism of his virtues. Thus pointed out to the Christian people, the power of St. Ignatius burst forth more than ever in favour of those who had recourse to him in confidence. On all sides people invoked this Saint who had such great credit with God, and for the unfortunates had such a compassionate heart. His relics enjoyed miraculous virtue; and the same can be said of the oil which burned before his altars and especially the water sanctified by the contact of his medal or his bones.

In a Notice published in Brussels, one can see with what many favours has been rewarded, for more than two centuries, the confidence of the faithful in this Blessed Water of St. Ignatius. The *Acta Sanctorum* mentions its use as early as

1599, when the plague was raging in Burgos in Spain; according to the testimony of the priests of this city, a great number of plague-stricken owed their cure to him. The same work attests that in 1712 the salutary effects of the water of St. Ignatius had made its use popular in Bohemia; incurable diseases yielded to this remedy taken with firm confidence in this powerful protector. The terrible invasions of cholera in Belgium, in the years of 1848, 1859, and 1866, also popularized this beneficial water there, the effectiveness of which was recognized mainly in Antwerp, Ghent, Bruges, Brussels, the faithful were eager to obtain it and were congratulated on having used it.[26]

In several places, this water is called the 'miraculous water', a name given to it in the past by the Protestants of Switzerland, who noticed it every day and even experienced its happy effects themselves.

A peculiarity of this devotion is too consoling to be omitted from mention. Numerous facts attest that the invocation of St. Ignatius is singularly effective in the two following circumstances where it is customary to have recourse to this great friend of childhood. First, when a mother finds herself in the apprehensions or anguish of a painful delivery, and second, when a desolate wife has lost all human hope of ever hearing herself called by the sweet name of mother. A recent example,

---

26   See the Appendix for some accounts of miracles
      attributed to the Holy Water of St. Ignatius.

quoted in the Notice, shows that St. Ignatius has lost none of his credit with God today, nor of his tender solicitude for souls so worthy of interest.

Without precluding the judgement of the Church on such favours, one may piously see in them an approval given by Heaven to the employment of this means; especially since His Holiness Pius IX has just consecrated the use of this water, determining by a special decree, on the date of the 30th of August 1866, the prayers that the Fathers of the Company of Jesus must recite to bless it.

At the request of the Father General of the Company of Jesus, His Holiness Pius IX consented that, in places where there are no Jesuit Fathers, the priests may, through their bishop, obtain from the Sacred Congregation of Rites the faculty to bless this water.

To experience the salutary effects of the Water of St. Ignatius, it might suffice to drink a little of it with confidence (i.e. with faith), or to make a lotion or sprinkling of it on the diseased part of the body, without restricting oneself to any exercise followed. However, most of the favours were obtained following one or more novenas, during which each day was added to the use of the Water the recitation of some prayers in honour of St. Ignatius.

One could, for nine days, recite in the morning and the evening before taking the Water, 3 Paters (3 Our Fathers), 3 Aves (3 Hail Marys), with the invocation; *'St. Ignatius, pray for us'*; or attend the Mass in honour of the Saint every day; or say the following prayers, which are translated from the authorized Latin formula for the blessing of this Water.

But since it is sin that has introduced death and all diseases into the world, nothing is more appropriate than to make a good confession during the novena, to receive Communion devoutly, thus recovering or strengthening the health of the soul at the same time as that of the body.

Let us add that confidence must always be accompanied by conformity to the will of God; let us know how to submit ourselves in a spirit of faith to Him, who, being our Father, only proposes things for the good of our souls, whether He accedes to our desires, or whether He refuses us certain favours.

The Prayer of Blessing over the Water

Latin and English:

In Latin -   Modus Benedicendi Aquam Sancti Ignatii Confessoris:

V. Adjutorium nostrum in nomine Domini.
R. Qui fecit coelum et terram.

V. Sit nomen Domini benedictum.

    R. Ex hoc nunc et usque in sæculum.

V Domine, exaudi orationem meam.

    R. Et clamor meus ad te veniat.

V. Dominus vobiscum,

    R. Et cum spiritu tuo.

Oremus: Domine sancte, Pater omnipotens, aeterne Deus, qui benedictionis tuae gratiam aegris infundendo corporibus, facturam tuam multiplici pietate custodis, ad invocationem nominis tui benignus assiste; ut, intercedente beato Ignatio confessore tuo, famulos tuos, ab aegritudine liberatos et sanitate donatos, dextera tua erigas, virtute confirmes, potestate tuearis, atque Ecclesiae tuae sanctae cum omni prosperitate restituas. Per Dominum, etc.

(Immergitur aquae numisma seu reliquiarium sancti Ignatii, et immersum tenetur atque ad finem hujus orationis.)

Benedic, ✠ Domine, hanc aquam, ut sit remedium salutare generi humano: et pet intercessionem beati Ignatii, cujus numisma in eam immergitur (vel reliquiae in eam immerguntur,) praesta ut quicumque ex ea sumpserint corporis sanitatem et animae tutelam percipiant. Per Chr. Etc.

(Educitur ex aqua numisma seu reliquiarium.)

Oremus: Deus, qui ad majorem tui nomis gloriam propagandam novo per beatum Ignaitum subsidio militantem Ecclesiam roborasti, concede ut ejus auxilio et imitatione certantes in terris coronari cum ipso mereamur in coelis. Per Dom....etc.

<u>English Translation</u>:

V. Our help is in the Name of the Lord.
R. Who made Heaven and earth.
V. Blessed be the name of the Lord.
R. Now and forever.
V. Lord, hear my prayer,
R. And let my cry come unto Thee.

Let us pray: Lord, Thou Who art infinitely holy, Father Almighty, Eternal God, Who, by pouring the grace of Thy blessing into the bodies of the sick, Thou Who guards Thy work with manifold tenderness, deign to lend a favourable ear to the invocation of Thy Name. Through the intercession of Blessed Ignatius, Thy confessor, may thy servant be freed from illness and given to health; may Thou raise them up by the aid of Thy right hand; supported with Thy power; guarded with Thy protection, and restored to Thy holy Church with every blessing. Through Jesus Christ Our Lord, (etc.)

(The medal or relic of St. Ignatius is then immersed in water, and is kept immersed until the end of the following prayer.)

Bless, ✠ Lord, this water, that it may be a salutary remedy for the human race. Grant that, through the intercession of blessed Ignatius, whose medal is immersed in it (or whose relics are immersed in it), that those who partake of it may obtain health of body and the protection of soul. Through Jesus Christ Our Lord, etc.

(The medal or reliquary is then taken out of the water.)

Let us pray: O God, who raised up St Ignatius of Loyola in your Church to further the greater glory of Thy Name, grant that, by his help, we may imitate him in fighting the good fight on earth and merit to receive with him a crown in heaven. Through our Lord Jesus Christ, Thy Son, Who lives and reigns with Thee in union with the Holy Ghost, One God, for ever and ever. Amen.

Official Decree of Approval and Use this Blessing

Sanctissimus Dominus noster Pius Papa IX, clement er deferens supplicibus votis Reverendissimi Patris Petri Beckx, Praepositi Generalis Societatis Jesu, a subscripto Sacrorum Rituum Congregationis Secretario relatis, suprascriptam formulam ad benedicendam aquam a sancto Ignatio confessore nuncupatam, a Sacra Rituum Congregatione diligenter revisam et correctam uti in superiori exemplari prostat, supreme auctoritate sua approbavit; indulsitque ut eadem formula in benedictione praedistae aquae uti valeant sacerdotes alumni Societatis ipsius. Quum autem memoratus Reverendissimus Pater Praepositus Generalis exquisiverit etiam ab eodem Sanctissim Domino nostro, ut iis in locis in quibus non extant domus Societatis suae, ad hanc benedictionem delegare valeat alios quoque sacerdotes, de consensu tamen Ordinarii dioecesani, Sanctitas Sua clementer annuit ut praefata benedictionis formula adhiberi possit in illis dioecesibus, quarum Ordinarii a Sacra Rituum Congregatione ejusdem extensionem petierint et pro iis tantum locis ubi non adsint domus Societatis Jesu. Contrariis non obstantibus quibuscumque.

Die 30a augusti 1866.

C. Episcopus Portuen. Et S. Rufinae, Card. Patrizi S.R.C. Praef.

Pro R. P. D. Dominico Bartolini Secretario, Josephus Ciccolini, substitutus.

(General Translation)[27]

Our most holy Lord Pius Pope IX, clemency bearing the vows of the Most Reverend Father Peter Beckx, Superior General of the Society of Jesus, reported by the undersigned Secretary of the Congregation of Sacred Rites, to use the above formula for blessing water called by Saint Ignatius the Confessor, carefully revised and corrected by the Congregation of Sacred Rites in the above copy he approved by his supreme authority; and he indulged that the priests, students of the Society himself, should be able to use the same formula in the blessing of the water provided. And since the aforementioned Most Reverend Father Superior General has also requested from the same Most Holy Lord, that in those places where there are no houses of his Society, he may also delegate other priests to this blessing, yet with the consent of the diocesan Ordinary, His Holiness graciously nods to the aforesaid formula of blessing it can be used in those dioceses whose Ordinaries have

---

27   Strange to see, Fr de Boylesve did not include a translation of the Latin decree of approval, I have attempted a translation despite my lack of skill in this language. Please note, the translation may be literal in places and therefore there may be errors.

requested the same extension from the Sacred
Congregation of Rites and only for those places
where there are no houses of the Society of Jesus.
Notwithstanding anything to the contrary.

August 30, 1866.

   C. Bishop of Portuen. And St. Rufinae, Card.
      Patrizi S.R.C. President

 By R. P. D. Dominic Bartolini Secretary,
Josephus Ciccolini, substitute.

ഇ ❖ ൟ

AD DEI
MA OR
N GL RI
M V M

The Spirit of St. Ignatius

According to the testimony of his historians, St. Ignatius loved his monks so sincerely, he looked upon them with such affable eyes, that he seemed entirely composed of charity and tenderness. He esteemed them all very much and always spoke of them with praise, from which it resulted: 1. that he did not easily suspect evil (of anyone); 2. that he was not too credulous in reports. "You my religious edify me," he said one day, "I am only scandalized by myself." To see his attentions and his cordiality, each imagined himself to be the best friend of his superior, not suspecting that another could be loved as much or more than himself.

To approach him and be welcomed by him, it not necessary to choose the 'favourable moment', nor to have recourse to any expedient. At all times, whether he was well or ill, he was accessible, in pain as in joy, in reverses as in successes. He listened to the end without interrupting. He invited anyone who approached him to come close, and if it was a priest, he immediately rose to do him honour. His greeting was so gracious, his word so benevolent, not only when he called, but when he was met unexpectedly, that one easily judged he carried all his children in his heart. His maxim was that a superior, conversing alone with his inferiors, should treat them with respect and love, like a father his married sons, and in the presence of strangers or other religious, with respect and kindness like an elder brother with his younger brothers.

If someone asked him something that he could not grant, he refused, but not without giving the reason for his refusal if prudence permitted.   If he granted it, he revealed the reasons for which he would have had the right to refuse; in this way, the one who received the favour requested withdrew happier, and the one who did not receive it withdrew less dissatisfied.

Before entrusting a job of any difficulty, he admonished the subject to collect himself before God and to consider; 1, if he was ready to do everything that would be ordered of him; 2, if he had more inclination for one job than for another; 3, if the choice is left to him, which would he prefer. "Man," he said, "fulfils his task better and longer, when it conforms to his tastes and aptitudes."

He never allowed himself a hard denomination or a risky reproach. A brother passing by his side with an air of distraction: "Brother Dominic," he said to him, "God has given you such great interior modesty, that you do not also show it exteriorly and in your eyes!"

If someone uttered an unmeasured word in front of him, he didn't say a word for the time being, but he made sure with a look or a gesture that the individual considered themselves warned. He absolutely refused to correct those religious who were absent and therefore incapable of defending themselves. He didn't even want to always take Father Polanque, his minister, a man as moderate as he was faithful, at his word regarding the account he gave him of the house according to his office. To cut short any false and malignant report, any preconceived and rash judgement, he only ever accepted written reports when the matter was of some gravity, "For, he said, one does not see what they say, but one sees well what they write."

A young novice, fatigued by the rule, was beginning to grow disgusted with his vocation: St. Ignatius, having known of it, allowed him to live for a few days as he pleased, rising, eating, walking about as he pleased. Touched by this kindness and a little relaxed, the novice was ashamed of his delicacy and asked for the common train again. Another novice, a noble Roman, had once been ordained to serve the stone masons publicly; St. Ignatius hearing it revoked the order, saying it was subjecting this young man to too severe a test.[28] Father Gonzalve having asked him if he could, by small presents, excite the young people to work: "Yes, yes," the Saint responded, "attract by small

---

28 Note, this is in reference to the stone workers, and not the secret society. St. Ignatius spared the nobleman of ministering among the workman as he came from a privileged life, and being thrown in with hard work possibly beyond his strength so soon might have tempted him to leave his vocation. He was charitably keeping in mind the young man's strengths and capabilities, and also his weaknesses.

presents, these children of the good God; I want it, I desire it." He himself distributed little by little to two brothers, still children and novices, jams that their mother had sent them. He allowed a novice to possess a beautiful crucifix for quite a long time as he had brought it from his family; then, when this novice had made progress in the spiritual life, said; "It is now time, my brother, that you must remove the crucifix from your hands to put it in your heart."[29]

He was seen imposing a three-day fast, accompanied by fervent prayers and groans before God, in order to obtain for one of his novices the deliverance of a temptation against their vocation. He spent the greater part of the night with another novice, knocking at the door of his heart, explaining to him, with that persuasion which accompanied all his words, the powerful reasons which were to hold him back, appalling or consoling him, making him alternately shed tears of fear and tears of repentance. When he discovered by a supernatural light that the real motive of the temptation (to leave their vocation) was a hidden sin, he put his finger on the wound, did not seek every means to bring about the confession, sometimes himself made the accusation of his faults, and did not hesitate to wake one of the

---

29 I.e. he did not demand the ornate crucifix be given up right away, he gave the novice time to grow stronger spiritually and therefore made it easier and much less painful for him break with his sentimental attachment to the possession later.

confessors of the house in the middle of the night so as not to put off until the next day what should restore peace to an unfortunate person.[30]

St. Ignatius was very concerned about the health of his disciples, especially those who worked for the benefit of souls, "considering that on their health usually depends the salvation of many, and that being dedicated to the apostolate, they must expend themselves in the service of God and neighbour." To provide the necessary, it happened to him he had to sell the crockery and .... [31] of the house. "The health of only one of my brothers, he said, is more precious to me than all the riches of the world, and God cannot abandon those who borrow for God." He wanted poverty to be remembered in liberality, and liberality in poverty never to be forgotten, curbing all the complacency that could lead to sin, but omitting none that could lead to virtue.

He wished to be informed first of the indispositions of his monks; he walked around the infirmary several times each night, and twice a day he asked the buyer if he had filled the doctor's prescriptions. If he encountered a sad illness, preoccupied with the patient's ills, he brought in novices skilled in music, and, to distract him, engaged them to sing fairy tales.

---

30   I.e. when he identified a need for confession, he did not pry or force, but accused himself of his own faults first to soften the heart of the troubled novice, then gently made confession available for him right away.

31 Unfortunately, the text is missing here.

During an illness that he had himself, he relieved himself of everything (all duties), except the solicitude of the infirmary. "Know," he said on one occasion, "that I love my brothers so much that I would like to know the number of flea bites suffered by them each night." He attributed this tenderness he felt for the sick to his own continual infirmities, and he thanked God for it.

Willingly he would bring guests or newcomers from their rooms to escort them to the refectory and place them near him. More than once, seeing a monk who did not like one dish, he was served another. When he ate with the community, he was the last to finish his meal, and if someone arrived after the others, he pushed the delicacy to the point of occupying himself with a small piece of bread to take away the embarrassment for the latecomer of having to eat alone.

In order to tighten the knots of charity among his scattered disciples and to make them taste as much as possible the sweetness of family life, he required that superiors and inferiors write him long and frequent letters about their situation, their work, their successes; then he made copies or made extracts which he sent to all the houses of the Company.

As St. Francis Xavier left for Portugal and the Indies, St. Ignatius wanted to know if this dear son had everything he needed for the trip. Realizing that he had no woollen waistcoat, he took his and gave it to him.

He himself accompanied those who left

Rome; for, adds Lancicius, one cannot imagine how much the inferior is sensitive to the politeness of a superior who does not part with him until the last moment, puts in his hand a pious object as a token of sadness at his parting and good memory, and still follows him with his eyes to renew his farewells.

Thus the heart of the good father was revealed down to the smallest detail.

Saint Ignatius of Loyola and
Allegories of the Four Continents

Canticle
St. Ignatius and the Company of Jesus

'No, no, I will not serve,'
 Says a menacing voice,
'Come, let us break the yoke.
In vain does helpless Rome
Recall once again the refrain of combat.'

(Chorus): God! When it comes to Thy glory,
We will sail against the waves;
The Cross ensures us victory;
Courage, onward, sailors.

Meanwhile from high above
God let the thunder gather
And His gaze seemed to ask the earth,
A voice repeats the victorious song:

(Chorus etc.)

Who is this young and handsome warrior!
Do you see him as he advances?
The high forehead, the ardent eye;
        how he runs and soars
Wherever a laurel is promised by peril?

(Chorus, etc.)

Why does this big heart have to
Be in love with the world and its glories?
Stop, Ignatius, hear the thundering storm,
And of the infernal breath you will brave the fury.

(Chorus etc.)

Upon these two standards gaze:
Two chiefs promise a crown;
 In Zion one reigns, in Babylon the other:
On Jesus, rests the glance of Ignatius.

(Chorus, etc.)

His eye measures the universe,
His heart embraces both worlds;
By his powerful voice he hovers over the waves:
Companions of Jesus, come then, cover the seas.

(Chorus, etc.)

Courage, vigorous oarsmen!
The flag of the vessel
Is the cross, and always will be,
        and you, faithful troop,
The generous refrain you will always repeat;

(Chorus, etc.)

Go forth, go forth, in the name of Jesus,
Go forth little Company,
Are you not afraid? Go always; your star is Mary!
Go over all the seas, and gather the elect.

(Chorus, etc.)

Drape together your flags,
Benedict, Guzman, Francis, Ignatius:
The century has spewed against you the menace,
Unite your voices and your labours against him.

(Chorus, etc.)

(Music may be found at Graff,
1, Rue de Mézières, Paris.)

ℰ❖ℛ

**Saints and Blesseds
of the Company of Jesus**[32]

St. Francis Xavier
St. Francis de Borgia
St. Jean-François Regis
S. François de Hieronymo
St. Louis de Gonzague
St. Stanislas Kostka
St. Paul Miki
St. John de Goto
St. James Kisaï

Bl. Alphonse Rodriquez.
Bl. PeterClaver.
Bl. John de Britto
Bl. Andrew Bobola
Bl. Peter Canisius
Bl. John Berchmans
Bl. Piere Le Févre
Bl. Ignatius d'Azévédo, and his 39 companions
Bl. James Andrada
Bl. Antony Suarez
Bl. Benedict de Castro
Bl. Francis de Magallanez
Bl. Jean Fernandez
Bl. Louis Correa
Bl. Emmanuel Rodriguez
Bl. Simon Lopez

---

32   Note: a number of blesseds have been canonised since.
     Also, this list is not exhaustive.

Bl. Emmanuel Fernandez
Bl. Alvare Mendez
Bl. Peter Nugnez
Bl. André Gonzalez
Bl. John de San-Martino
Bl. Gonzalve Henriquez
Bl. Didace Perez
Bl. Ferdinand Sanchez
Bl. Francis Perez-Godoï
Bl. Antony Correa
Bl. Emmanuel Pacheco
Bl Nicolas Diniz
Bl. Alexis Delgado
Bl. Mark Caldeira
Bl. Joannin San-Juan
Bl. Emmanuel Alvarez
Bl Francis Alvarez
Bl. Dominic Fernandez
Bl Gaspard Alvarez
Bl Adhemar Vaz
Bl John de Marjoga
Bl. Alfonsus de Vaena
Bl Antony Fernandez
Bl Etienne Zuraire
Bl Peter Fontoura
Bl. Gregory Escribano
Bl. John de Zafra
Bl. John de Baeza
Bl. Blaize Ribéra
Bl. John Fernandez
Bl. Simon Acosta

Bl. Charles Spinola
Bl. Jean-B. Machado
Bl. Didace Carvalho
Bl. Michael Carvalho
Bl. Paul Navarro
Bl. Denis Fugixima
Bl. Peter Onizuki
Bl. Léonard Chimura
Bl. Francis Pachéco
Bl. John -B. Zola
Bl. Balthasar de Torres
Bl Gaspard Sandamatzu
Bl. Peter Rinxei
Bl. Paul Chinsuche
Bl. Jean Chinsaco
Bl. Michael Tozo
Bl. Vincent Caun
Bl. Antony Ixida
Bl. Thomas Tzugi
Bl. Michael Nagaxima
Bl. Sébastien Chumura
Bl. Antony Kiuni
Bl. Peter Sampo
Bl. Michael Xumpo
Bl. Gonzalve Fuzaï
Bl Thomas Acafoxi
Bl. Louis Cavara
Bl. John Kingocou
Bl. Ambroise Fernandez
Bl. Camille Costanzo
Bl. Augustin Ota
Bl Jérôme de Angelis
Bl. Simon Jempo

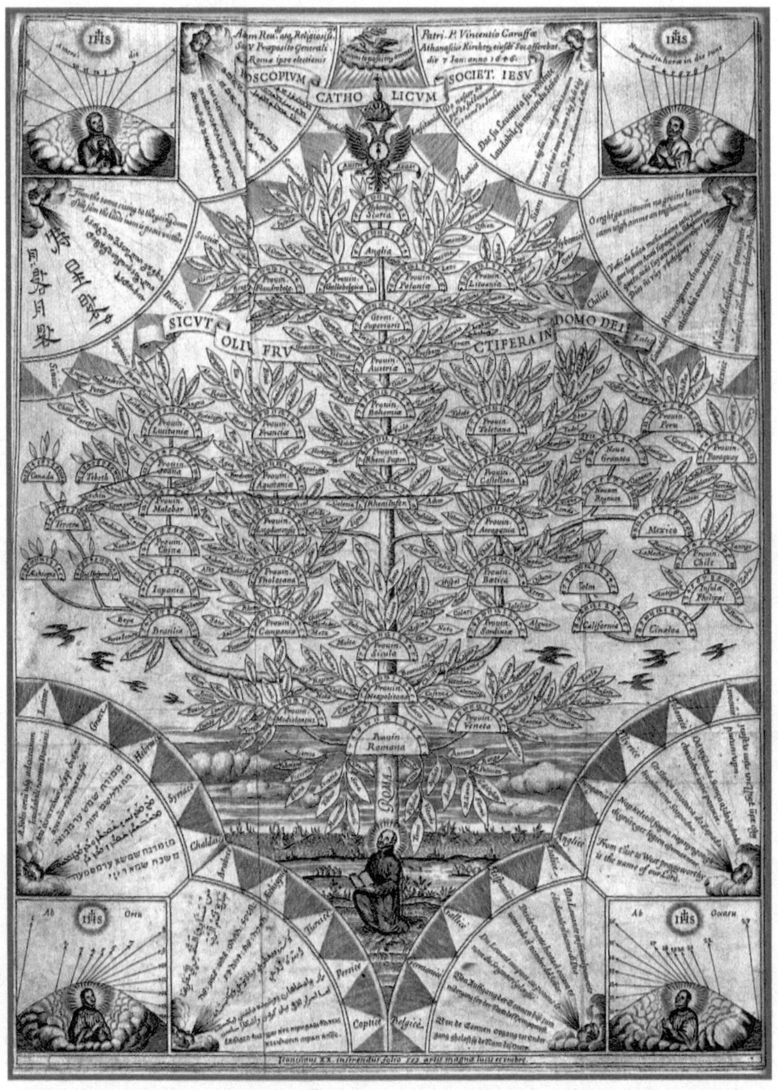

A family tree of the provinces and colleges of the Jesuit order, with horological markings to show the time in each location relative to noon in Rome.

Engraving after A. Kircher, 1646

APPENDIX

<u>Biography of St. Ignatius of Loyola by Fr. Francis Xavier Weninger, (1876)</u>[33]

St. Ignatius, the glorious founder of the Society of Jesus, and the unweary labourer for the greater glory of God and the salvation of souls, was born of noble parents in Biscay, a province of Spain, in the castle of Loyola, from which he took his name. His birth took place in 1491, in the same century in which Martin Luther, the well-known heretic, was born, who with Calvin, born in 1506, persecuted the Catholic Church and endeavoured to destroy it entirely. God, according to a papal declaration, always watching over His holy Church, would oppose Ignatius to these two new heretics, that through him, and through the Society founded by him, their erroneous doctrines might be thoroughly refuted, and the Catholic faith have powerful protectors, as, in former days, He had opposed Arius by St. Athanasius, Nestorius by St. Cyril, Pelagius by St. Augustine, and other heretics by other apostolic men.

Ignatius, chosen by God for so important a work, was endowed with great natural gifts, possessed a comprehensive mind, and early

---

33 Source: https://catholicharboroffaithandmorals.com

exhibited wonderful abilities and tact, with unusual wisdom and strength of soul. All his aspirations were lofty, and nothing vulgar or low could attract him. Soon perceiving his talents, his parents sent him, after he had been carefully instructed in the Catholic faith, to the Court of King Ferdinand of Castile, where he was educated with the pages, and was taught all that was supposed befitting his rank. In riper years, he entered the army, hoping to become famous by his valour. In 1521, an opportunity was offered to give a proof of his courage. The king had entrusted to him the defence of the city of Pampeluna (Pamplona), which was besieged by the French. Ignatius acted with all the prudence and caution of an old and experienced warrior. But Providence so ordered, that the wall upon which Ignatius stood, bravely defending the fortress, was struck by a cannonball, and a fragment of stone severely injured one of his limbs, while at the same time the ball rebounding, bruised his foot so badly, that he sank unconscious to the ground. The French were soon in possession of the fortress, but they treated their heroic prisoner with the greatest kindness, and sent him, a few days later, on a litter, to the Castle of Loyola. Here Ignatius became so ill, that it was deemed necessary to give him the last sacraments. The thread on which his life hung: was so slender that the physicians all agreed that there was no hope for him, if before midnight the symptoms should not change.

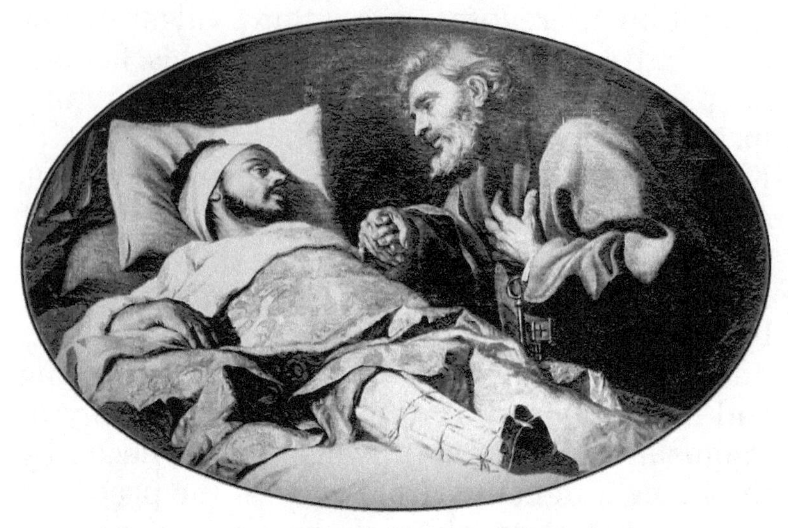

The Most High did not wish to call Ignatius out of life, and had brought him to this state only to make him disgusted with the world, and so lead him to a holier warfare. Therefore, on the eve of the feast of the Apostles St. Peter and St, Paul, God sent the Prince of the Apostles, to whom Ignatius had been greatly devoted from his early youth, to restore him to health. Appearing to Ignatius during his sleep, St. Peter looked tenderly at him, and touching his wounds, took from him all pain, and thus saved him from the danger of death.

But nevertheless, it was the will of God that Ignatius should keep his bed a considerable time, in order to regain his strength. To pass the time, he asked for something to read; but, by special providence, none of the romances he desired were to be found, and in their stead, two devout books were brought to him, one containing the "Life of Christ", and the other the "Lives of the Saints". Ignatius, little inclined to read them, took them for want of others, and at first only looking into them, soon became, by the grace of God, so deeply interested in them that, meditating on the acts of Christ and the Saints, he repented of his past idle life, and resolved, thenceforth, to follow their steps, and to serve God alone. Rising during the night, he cast himself before an image of the Blessed Virgin, begging of her the grace to be accepted into her service and that of her beloved Son, and to remain in it until the end of his days.

Hardly was his prayer finished, when suddenly a terrible noise was heard, the house was shaken as by an earthquake, and the windows were shattered. St. Ignatius regarded this as a sign that his prayer was heard, and exhibited more joy than fear. The Evil One, hereupon, endeavoured, by a thousand representations and apprehensions, to make him abandon his determination, and pressed him with the most dangerous temptations. But Ignatius again sought refuge with the divine Mother, and addressed her in the words of the

Holy Church: "Show thyself a Mother." The Divine Mother appeared to him with her heavenly Child, and animating him to persevere, she assured him of her assistance. After this comforting vision, all his temptations ended, and all his thoughts were directed towards the regulation of his new life. As soon as he was sufficiently recovered, he, under some pretext, left the house of his father and repaired to Montserrat, where a miraculous image of the Blessed Virgin drew crowds of pilgrims. There he made his general confession amid a flood of tears, and received, with the greatest devotion, the Blessed Sacrament. After this, he gave his horse to the monastery, and hung his sword near the altar of the Blessed Virgin, as a sign that henceforth he would no longer serve the world but God only. Having bestowed his costly garments on a beggar, he clothed himself as a poor pilgrim, and remained, as a newly-enrolled soldier of the highest of all generals, all night long before the altar of the Mother of Mercy, in fervent prayer.

The next day, which was the feast of the Annunciation of our Lady, he left early and betook himself to Manresa, which is three miles from Montserrat, and going to the hospital which was there, he served the sick with the most tender devotion.

As soon, however, as he detected that they began to esteem him for his charity and other pious deeds, he secretly left and went into a mountain cave, five or six hundred yards off,

in which he led an extremely austere and penitential life. He daily spent seven hours on his knees, praying and weeping on account of his sins. He fasted continually except on Sundays, when he partook of the food of angels. Water and the bread which he received as alms, was his only nourishment. He always wore a hair-shirt, which was fastened round his loins by small chains. He scourged himself three times daily, often unto blood. The bare ground was his bed, and he never took more than a few hours' rest, passing the remainder of the night in meditation on death and the Passion of Christ.

By long continuation of this austere life, his body became so emaciated and weak, that he was found more than once, lying more dead than alive on the road to Manresa, whither he used to go to assist at Holy Mass. Some friends advised him not to be so severe with himself; but he said: "Oh! let me suffer this trifle in order to secure my salvation." Satan also tried to dissuade him from his austerities, and as he could not succeed, he took, by the permission of the Almighty, the form of a virtuous man, and going to the holy penitent, said, that it was not possible to continue long such extreme mortifications, and that he should therefore moderate them somewhat. "Unhappy man," said he, "you may still live seventy years; and have you the courage to spend so long a time in such penance and severity?" Ignatius replied: "Can you promise me one single day of the many years of which you speak?" With these words, he brought the spirit of lies to shame, and drove him away. God permitted also this holy penitent to be tormented with the most harassing scruples. To overcome these, he resolved to abstain from all food and drink until he was free from them, as he had read that a certain Saint had used this remedy in a similar case. Seven days he passed without partaking of any nourishment; but his confessor, on hearing of it, commanded him to take his usual sustenance. Ignatius obeyed, and was from that moment not only released from his scruples, but obtained also from God an especial gift to free others from them.

Many other special graces did the Almighty bestow upon Ignatius in the first year of his conversion, which space does not permit us to relate. But there is one thing which we cannot omit to mention: it is that, during the year of penance at Manresa, Ignatius wrote that wonderful book of "Spiritual Exercises", which has been recommended by the most learned and the most holy men, as the path, pointed out by heaven itself, to conversion, to spiritual perfection and holiness. The Apostolic See has praised and confirmed it, and the spiritual benefits which have been derived from it, and are still to this hour derived from it, are inexpressibly great. But as it is known that Ignatius, when he wrote this book, was as yet without learning, it must be concluded that he was inspired by God to give those instructions, by virtue of which he, and, later, the sons of his Order, worked real miracles of conversion in so many different places and persons. During this penitential year,

St. Ignatius in the Holy Land

the heart of Ignatius was filled with an intense desire to visit the Holy Land, not only for the purpose of seeing those places which have been hallowed by the presence of our Saviour, but also in the hope of converting the Mohammedans, and of giving his life for the true faith, in that land where our beloved Redeemer gave His for our welfare.

This voyage was undertaken in the greatest poverty and with deep devotion, and the holy places visited with a true spirit of ardent piety and reverence. As, however, the ecclesiastics, who resided there, dissuaded him from remaining long, and Ignatius himself recognized that, to gain his aim in life, which was to further the salvation of souls, he needed learning, he returned to Europe, and began at Barcelona, when 33 years of age, to study the rudiments of the Latin grammar with the boys in the public school. He continued his studies at different places and finished them at Paris, where he received the title of Doctor of Divinity. The trials, dangers, persecutions, disgraces, wrongs and calumnies he suffered, as well in his travels as during the years of his studies, would be too long to relate here. On his return from the Holy Land, he was seized by the Spaniards, who were at war with France, and was at first taken for a spy, and afterwards for a fool, and thus most disgracefully treated. By a few words, he could have escaped these insults; but he was silent and bore it all patiently, for the love of Christ, who just then had appeared to Him. At several places where he studied, or through which he travelled, he was apprehended by order of the authorities, and cast into prison; as at Alcala, Salamanca and Venice. The only cause of this cruel treatment was that, wherever the holy man was, he showed solicitude for the salvation of others, and converted many by his pious discourses, explanation of the Christian doctrine and his own "Spiritual Exercises". Many he persuaded to leave the world, others he led to a quiet Christian life. For this he was suspected of disseminating false doctrines and corrupting men under the appearance of piety. But as often as he was

St. Ignatius in Spain

examined, he was found guiltless, and requested to continue in his zeal.

At Paris, where he had recalled many young men from an idle and sinful life to a better and more useful one, it was resolved to whip him in public, as a corrupter of youth. When, however, the director of the school had recognized his innocence, he publicly and on his knees asked pardon of the Saint, and praised, in the highest terms, his zeal in leading souls in the path of salvation. To speak of God and of heavenly things had become a second nature to him, so that those who knew not his name, called him the man of spiritual conversation, or the man who was constantly looking up to heaven. He reformed a convent near Barcelona, the inmates of which stood in very ill repute. This drew upon him the vengeance of certain persons, who had been, at his suggestion, excluded from the house, and who, one day, lay in wait for him and beat him most unmercifully, threatening to treat him still worse, if he did not cease preaching at the convent. Ignatius was not in the least deterred by this from his good work. His enemies then hired two ruffians to kill him. These set upon him and treated him in a most brutal manner, whilst the Saint, with eyes raised to heaven, prayed God to forgive them. They left him weltering in his blood, supposing they had killed him. He, however, recovered, and no sooner were his wounds healed, than he again went to the convent in order to strengthen the nuns to perseverance in virtue. When someone tried to dissuade him from going, on account of the danger, he said: "What can be more pleasing to me than to die for love of Christ and my neighbours?" Not satisfied with his personal labours for the salvation of souls, he resolved to seek such men as would join him with all the power of their minds, to labour for the same object. He succeeded in uniting to himself nine students of the University of Paris, all of whom possessed great knowledge and were eminent for their talents. Among them was Francis Xavier, afterwards so celebrated as the Apostle of the

Indies. Ignatius, by his "Spiritual Exercises", led them all to virtue and sanctity, and inspired them with the fervent desire to devote themselves to the salvation of souls and to the honour of God.

In 1534, on the feast of the Assumption of our Lady, Ignatius and his companions went to a Chapel, dedicated to the Blessed Virgin, on Montmartre, near Paris, and after they had received Holy Communion, they all made a vow to renounce the world and go to Jerusalem to convert the heathen. If, however, they were unable, after waiting one year, to make their way to Palestine, they vowed that they would go to Rome, throw themselves at the feet of the Holy Father, and offer their services in whatever he might deem most beneficial for the salvation of souls. On account of a war between the Turks and the Venetians, they were unable to make their pilgrimage to Palestine; and hence, in fulfilment of their vow, they went to Rome. When Ignatius and the two companions who were with him had reached a place called La Storta, near Rome, the Saint went into a chapel nearby to say his prayers. His fervour was such that, in an ecstasy, he saw the Heavenly Father and beside Him His Son bearing the Cross. He heard the Heavenly Father commend him with loving words to His Son, putting him and his companions under His protection. The Divine Son manifested His pleasure at this Divine command, and turning to Ignatius, said: "I will favour you at Rome." With this the vision ended, but the inner comfort which Ignatius and his companions, to whom he related it, derived from it, departed not, but remained in their hearts.

As soon as Ignatius had arrived in Rome, he threw himself at the feet of the Holy Father and offered the services of himself and his companions, for such spiritual labour as he might wish them to do in any part of the world. The Pope received them with pleasure, and having had sufficient proofs of their virtue and learning, he sent some of them to those places where he thought they would do the most good. Ignatius remained with the rest at Rome, and at first instructed young and old in the Christian doctrine; but later, he began to preach for the reformation of morals and exhorted the people to a more frequent use of the holy Sacraments. It cannot be denied that the custom of instructing children in the Christian doctrine, and also the frequent reception of the holy Eucharist, which was at that period greatly neglected, were again revived, or at least increased by St. Ignatius and his companions. To preserve this improvement and these advantages for future times, and to increase them still more, St. Ignatius resolved to found a new Order, whose members should labour for the spiritual well-being of men. He disclosed his intentions to the Pope, and having written, by his permission, certain rules, presented them to his Holiness for approval. After many difficulties, the holy desires of Ignatius were at length fulfilled, and thus was founded a new Order, under the name of the Society of Jesus, which in the year 1540 was first

sanctioned by Paul III, afterwards by several other Popes, and was also confirmed by the Council of Trent. This Order demands of its members, besides the usual three vows of perpetual poverty, chastity and obedience, a vow to instruct youth, and requires of the Professed another vow, of special obedience to the Pope, by which they are bound to go, even without money, whithersoever the Pope may send them to labour for the salvation of souls. Ignatius was chosen as General by the members of the new Order, but he did not accept the office until he was commanded to do so by his confessor after having long consulted with God in prayer. He administered his office with admirable wisdom and strength of character, and to the immeasurable benefit of the entire Christian world, until his death.

Although remaining at Rome, he sent his disciples into other cities and lands, after having instructed them carefully in all that pertained to the salvation of souls and to the manner of leading them to God. Above all, he recommended entire self-abnegation, after the example of Christ, Who has said: "Whoever will follow me, must deny himself." Hence he often said these important words: "Conquer thyself." St. Francis Xavier, who frequently made use of this expression, was asked why he did so? He answered: "Because I learned it from our Father Ignatius." Ignatius further endeavoured to lead his disciples to acquire true virtue, especially a fervent love of God and of their neighbours. In this, as in all other virtues, he was a shining example to them all. According to the testimony of the Apostolic See, he had acquired the most perfect control over his inclinations. He also taught the members of the Order to be solicitous for the cleanliness and beauty of the house of God, for the conversion of heretics and heathens, for the promotion of virtue among Catholics, for the instruction of the ignorant, especially of children in the mysteries of the faith; for the frequent use of the Sacraments; for the increase of the veneration of the Blessed Virgin; and, in a word, for everything that could advance the honour of God and the salvation of souls.

The members of the Order faithfully obeyed his directions. The fame of the great good that these holy men did, induced many kings and princes to invite them into their states. Among these, the first was John III, King of Portugal, who, through his Ambassadors at Rome, demanded seven of the Fathers of the Society of Jesus. At this request, Ignatius sighed deeply and said: "If the king requires seven of my brethren, how many will remain for other countries?" These words show how zealous he was in his thoughts and wishes. As the number of his religious was small, at that time, and as he would, moreover, send none who were not well-grounded in learning and virtue, instead of seven, he sent but two; but those two did more than could have been expected of seven.

They were Simon Rodriguez and Francis Xavier, the latter of whom, on account of his having converted many thousands of heathens and performed many miracles, is known and honoured all over the Christian world. The good which was done by the holy efforts of these two men, induced the king to found the first college for the Society of Jesus, at Goa, the capital of India, and soon after, another at Coimbra in Portugal, which, in the course of time, supplied many places with apostolic labourers. While thus the disciples of St. Ignatius untiringly laboured to win souls for Heaven in Portugal, India, and other countries, the Holy Father employed equally well those who were with him in Rome. All that he had taught his companions about decorating the house of God, converting the heretics, and instructing the Catholics, as before related, he practised at Rome, without abating his zeal. "The world seemed too small for him," said Gregory XV. No labour, no danger, could deter him, where the salvation of even a single soul was concerned. "If I could die a thousand deaths in one day," said he on one occasion, "I would willingly do so to save a single soul." At another time he was heard to say, that if he had the choice either to die immediately with the assurance of his salvation, or without this assurance to live and to have an opportunity to gain a soul for Heaven, he would rather remain upon earth and save that soul than die immediately and go to Heaven. These words display the love of St. Ignatius towards his neighbour and his zeal for the spiritual welfare of men.

No less was this manifested in his works;

and it can be truly said that there was no man, whatever his race or station, for whose welfare he did not labour either personally or through the members of his order. With the greatest love and solicitude, he instructed children in the Christian doctrine, even when he was general of the order, and bound all its members to do the same. He founded public schools in various places, where youth was instructed in virtue and learning without any compensation. People of all ages and conditions were animated by his pious discourses, and especially by his "Spiritual Exercises", to fervour in the service of God, and were led not only to repentance for their sins, but to the practice of the highest virtue. For the welfare of orphans and of children who had been abandoned by their parents, he established in Rome two houses where they were taken care of and instructed until they were able to take care of themselves. For single women, who on account of their poverty were in danger of sin, he founded the Asylum of St. Catharine, where they had a home until they either entered a convent or were provided with a dowry. Another house was founded for women who were willing to abandon their wicked life and do penance. In it they were maintained and instructed. God only knows how many sins the holy man prevented by the foundation of these houses, and how much good he thus occasioned. It is true that some who had been reclaimed, returned to their old course of life, and the Saint was told that he should not waste his efforts upon them. But he answered:

St. Ignatius Preaching

"It does not seem to me that my care and labour have been lost, even if such persons return to their former vices. It is much if I prevent them from offending God only for a single night."

His solicitude extended even to the hardened Jews; their conversion was an object of great concern to him, and God blessed his efforts in their behalf with such signal success that he baptised forty of them in one year. He also established a house where those who had renounced Judaism were received and kept until they were thoroughly instructed in the Christian religion and baptised. The solicitude which the Saint manifested toward Germany, which was at that time in great danger of entirely forsaking the true faith, must not be forgotten. For the salvation of that country, he not only offered many prayers, penances and masses, but also ordered that all the priests of the Society should offer the holy sacrifice once every month, and all those who were not priests, should say certain prayers for the same intention. This ordinance is still kept. Besides this, he instituted, amidst infinite difficulties, the German College, which is still in existence in Rome, and in which young Germans are educated for the priesthood and prepared for the missions, in order that when their education is completed and they return to their homes, they may be able to protect the Catholic religion, convert the heretics, and by their good example, induce all to live virtuously. Martin Chemnitz, a well known Lutheran, wrote in regard to this College, that if the Society of Jesus had done but this, it could be called the destroyer of the reformed religion. St. Ignatius further manifested his sympathy with oppressed Germany, by sending several apostolic men to Cologne, Mayence, and other cities, who bravely opposed the heretics, and animated the Catholics to fidelity to their church. Melancthon, the assistant of Luther, said himself, that by the power of these men, the dissemination of the new (reformation) gospel was greatly hindered. When he perceived that the number of the Society daily increased, he cried out with grief: "Oh! Woe, woe! How will it be with the new gospel? The whole world will be filled with Jesuits!"

The Evil One, the founder and protector of all heresies, seemed to think the same; for he used his utmost endeavours to interfere with St. Ignatius in his most holy efforts. He instigated some to accuse, not only the Saint, but the whole Society, of the most hideous vices, and to persecute them whenever there was the slightest opportunity. There is not to be found an Order which, during its whole existence, has had to suffer such bitter persecution, and has been so slandered, so unjustly dealt with by the heretics, and even by some who called themselves Catholics, as the Order founded by St. Ignatius. But never was the Saint seen depressed about his personal persecutions; and the attacks which were directed against the whole Order he bore with great cheerfulness, as he concluded that as Satan was the author of them, he must have suffered some severe loss through the labours of the Society. On the contrary, when one day he was told that in a certain country, the members of his Order had nothing to suffer, he became very thoughtful, and said that he feared they were negligent in doing their duty, since they were not persecuted. He also prophesied that the Society of Jesus would always have the glory of being persecuted by the enemies of Christ and of the holy church. He frequently recalled the words of Christ: "If they have persecuted Me, they will persecute you."

The greater and more frequent the persecutions were, the more the Society increased, and the more extended was its usefulness among the faithful, the heretics and the heathens, to the indescribable consolation of its founder. Pope Marcellus II said that, since the days of the Apostles, he had never read of any one whose labours God had blessed with such abundant fruit during his life time, as those of St. Ignatius. The holy founder lived long enough to see his Order spread in all parts of the world, divided into twelve provinces, with more than one hundred colleges and houses. He heard how, by the unwearying labours of the Fathers, whole nations were converted from their idolatry to the true faith, numberless heretics brought back to the Church, and everywhere Catholics were strengthened in that faith, without which there is no salvation. He himself heard and saw how youth was carefully instructed in the Catholic religion, in the fear of God, and in all branches of knowledge; and how the people in general were animated to greater piety, to the more frequent use of the Holy Sacraments and all Christian virtues. He heard of the many miracles wrought by St. Francis Xavier, and other Apostolic men, in testimony to the true faith. He had the happiness of hearing that some members of his Order had heroically given their blood for the faith of Christ; and from every land he received news of the good which his children were incessantly doing for the honour of God and the salvation of souls. All this filled the heart of the holy man with inexpressible joy, as he desired nothing more fervently than that the Almighty might be known and honoured by all men. He was frequently heard to exclaim: "Oh God! that all men might know and love Thee."

Meanwhile his own soul burned with the desire to see, face to face, the God Whom he loved as his highest good. This desire grew to such an extent that the mere thought of death, or a glance at heaven, drew tears from his eyes, and made him disgusted with the whole world. Often, while looking up at the sky, he would cry out: "Oh! how I despise the world, when I look up to Heaven." He begged God to free his soul from the fetters of mortality. God heard his prayer. A fever seized him, and although the physicians pronounced it not dangerous, Ignatius knew that it was a messenger to call him away. He asked for the last Sacraments and devoutly received them. When evening came, he called one of the oldest Fathers of the Order, and sent him to ask for the Holy Father's last blessing and a plenary indulgence. He passed the night in an almost continual ecstasy, until an hour after sunrise, when, with eyes raised to heaven, and with the sacred names of Jesus and Mary on his lips, he ended his life, on July 31st, 1556, in the 64th year of his age. At the same hour when this took place, the Saint, arrayed in bright, shining light, appeared to a pious widow, named Margaret Gigli, at Bologna, and announced to her his death. The unexpected death of the great founder filled Rome with mourning, and everywhere was heard the lamentation: "The holy man is dead." Many did not hesitate to honour him as a Saint immediately, and ask his intercession with the Almighty. The resting place of his holy relics was twice changed. At the first interment, an eminent servant of the Almighty heard heavenly music during two days; at the second, many saw bright stars upon his shrine.

Holy men and women, who lived at the time of St. Ignatius, admired and praised the Saint and the Society he founded. St. Philip Neri, who lived at Rome, said that he had seen the countenance of Ignatius, several times, resplendent with a heavenly light. In all doubts and fears, he resorted to St. Ignatius for counsel and comfort. To two members of the Society, whom he met one day, he said: "You are sons of a great father, to whom I owe much; he taught me the science of prayer." After the Saint's death, Philip sent to the tomb to commend to him his cares, and according to his own words, received marvellous comfort and assistance. St. Francis Xavier esteemed the Saint so highly while he still lived, that he called him the beloved father of his soul, and a Saint. He cut the name of St. Ignatius from a letter which he had received from him, placed it in a reliquary and carried it about him, and wrought many miracles with it. He always wrote to him on his knees, as a sign of great reverence for him, and read the letters he received from him in the same manner. I must omit the praise bestowed on St. Ignatius by other Saints, as, St. Francis of Sales, St. Charles Borromeo, St. Cajetan, St. Andrew Avellino, St. Thomas of Villanova, St. Teresa, St. Mary Magdalen of Pazzi, and many others. The pious Louis of Granada, a Dominican, who lived at the time that St. Ignatius and his order were bitterly persecuted, showed himself a warm friend and powerful protector and admirer of both until his death. Neither shall I mention here what many Popes, bishops and other high dignitaries of the Church have said in praise of the Society of Jesus, nor repeat the high commendations given by crowned heads and great statesmen, although it might add greatly to the glory of the holy founder.

We will only consider somewhat more attentively the words of the Roman Calendar of the Saints. It states that the Saint was remarkable for holiness and miracles. Much is contained in these few words. Ignatius was remarkable for his holiness. The heroic virtues, which so brilliantly shone in him, are a proof of this; his firm and intense faith, his unwavering trust in God; his fervent love of the Saviour and of his neighbour; his tender affection for the passion and death of Christ; his filial devotion to the Virgin Mother; his constant self-abnegation; his perfect resignation to the Divine Will; his invincible patience, admirable meekness, deep humility, and insatiable zeal to labour for the honour of the Most High, and to save souls for Heaven. Especial instances of all these virtues are to be found in the book which treats of the devotion of the Ten Wednesdays in honour of St. Ignatius.[34]

Ignatius was also remarkable for his miracles. God worked many wonders through him during his life-time. One of his disciples who was dangerously sick, was healed by embracing him; another was cured of epilepsy. He relieved a noble matron from the Evil Spirit of whom she had been possessed four years, and healed several others of different maladies. He even restored life to a young man in Barcelona who had hung himself in despair and who was pronounced dead by all who saw him. God wrought still more miracles at the intercession of his faithful servant, after his death. In the process of his canonization we find two hundred miracles, which were tested by the ecclesiastical authorities and were found to rest on the authority of incontestable witnesses under oath. After the canonization their number was still increased. During his life also many other gifts and graces were granted him by God, such as the gift of tears; the gift of reading the hearts of others; the spirit of prayer which he possessed in so eminent a degree, that he often fell into ecstasies which lasted several days, and finally the gift of prophecy and revelations. It is known

---

34   Strangely, the text here says Ten Wednesdays, when the original devotion according to Fr de Boylesve should be Ten Sundays.

that he said to a youth at Barcelona, who desired to follow him and live in poverty: "You will remain in the world and become a lawyer, and the father of several children, one of whom will, in your place, enter the Order which God will found through me, His unworthy servant." At Antwerp he said to a merchant: "There will come a time when you will found a College in your country for the members of the Order which God will establish through me, His unworthy servant." All this took place exactly as he had foretold. The number of the revelations and visions with which he was blessed is very large.

Besides the visit of St. Peter, the Blessed Virgin and Our Lord, mentioned in the above pages, it is known that Christ appeared several times to him, at Manresa, during his year of penance; and also later during his holy life. The Blessed Virgin also appeared to him in like manner, especially at the time when he wrote his book of the "Spiritual Exercises". The Roman Breviary asserts that he was so enlightened by the grace of God, that he used to say, that if there were no gospel, he would be ready to die for his faith on the evidences which the Almighty had revealed him at Manresa. In one of his ecstasies, so much was revealed to him of the incomprehensible mystery of the Holy Trinity, that he wrote a book which excited the most profound astonishment of all learned men. At another time, the happy death of two of his companions was revealed to him. The first was made known to him whilst he was at Monte

Cassino, where, during his prayers, he saw the soul of Father Hozes, surrounded by a heavenly splendour, carried by angels into Heaven. The second was when on his way to say mass for his sick disciple at St. Peter's Church, in Rome, suddenly stopping in his walk, he looked fixedly up to Heaven, then turning to go home, he said: "Let us go home, for our Father Coduri has departed." From this it was concluded that he had seen the soul of the dead ascending to heaven.

To the visions which St. Ignatius had of others, I will add one that another had of him. At Cologne, on the Rhine, lived Leonard Kessel, a priest of the Society of Jesus, who had an intense desire to see St. Ignatius, who at that time resided at Rome. He begged permission to go, for this purpose, to Rome, which, however, was not granted him. While one day praying in his room, his holy Father Ignatius suddenly stood before him, and after having for some time kindly discoursed with him, as suddenly disappeared. All this proves that Ignatius was indeed remarkable for holiness, miracles and other divine gifts. In conclusion, I will explain why St. Ignatius is always represented in priestly robes, with the most holy name of Jesus on his breast and a book in his hand. His priestly robes denote that he was, in his time, an ornament to the priesthood, and eminently sanctified this dignity. It is further a sign of the great devotion with which the Saint said Mass. He offered the Holy Sacrifice of the Mass, for the first time on

Christmas-night, at Rome, before the manger of Our Lord, after eighteen months of preparation. It was on that occasion and frequently afterwards, that during Holy Mass, bright rays of light surrounded him, that he was raised from the ground, and his face suffused with tears of devotion. The more to satisfy his ardour, he generally said Mass in the chapel of the house, passing a whole hour in the act, during which he frequently fell into ecstasy, and had the grace of seeing Christ visible in the Host. The rapture was so intense, that it was feared his veins would burst, and he had often to be carried to his room in a state of exhaustion. He passed two hours in prayer before and after mass, whenever the duties of his office permitted.

The name of Jesus on his breast, is an evidence of the great love he bore for the Saviour. This and no other name would he give to his order, that its members might never forget how Christ laboured and suffered, and be thus encouraged to shrink from no labour for the Most High, to fear no danger, no persecution nor even death in the pursuance of that which had become their sacred duty. The Saint used to say that nothing could more effectually give us courage to endure, than the remembrance of this Holy Name. By the book which he holds in his hand, are designated the Rules which he wrote for his society, and which have been pronounced, by those able to judge, a most perfect piece of human wisdom. While he was writing this book, the Blessed Virgin appeared to him several times, and almost dictated what he wrote. The Council of Trent called it a pious Institution, approved by the Apostolic See, in which there was nothing to be altered. Pope Julius III said, in a Bull, that there was nothing in the Institute of the Society of Jesus, that was not pious and holy. Pope Paul III who was the first to approve and confirm the Society, when he was informed of the praiseworthy deeds which its members, in accordance with its rules, had performed, exclaimed: "The finger of God is here!" The words: "To the greater glory of God," which are read in the book, are those which St. Ignatius was wont to use, and they express the whole aim of his Rules which is no other than the advancement of the honour of God and the salvation of souls.

Practical Considerations

You will find much in the life of St. Ignatius which may serve you for instruction and example; and I will, in a few words, aid you to find some of the principal points.

I. The reform and holiness of the Saint began by reading a devout book, the *Lives of the Saints*. As I told you elsewhere, the reading of pious books, especially the *Lives of the Saints*, is of very great spiritual benefit; while the reading of a wicked work does intense harm. The vices and consequent damnation of many are the effects of reading dangerous books; while the holiness and final salvation of others, had their beginning in the lessons received while reading pious books. Judge from this in which direction your duty lies.

II. The purpose of all the actions of St. Ignatius was to promote the glory of God and the salvation of souls, and as he sought in everything only the glory of God, he always selected what was agreeable, nay most agreeable to Him. To do that which is always most pleasing to the Almighty, has always been the aim and distinguishing feature of all great saints on earth. To do only what is pleasing to God and to avoid that which is displeasing to Him, is the duty of every Christian.   To avoid only mortal sin, is the sign of a very indifferent man, who neither loves God, nor is concerned about his salvation. Among which of these will you be ranked? Endeavour to have a place among the first, and do nothing except what you are convinced is pleasing to the Almighty, and avoid all that you know is displeasing to His Majesty. Perform all your works for the honour of God and the salvation of your soul.

III. St. Ignatius was called the man who always spoke of God and looked constantly to Heaven. Of that of which the heart is full, the mouth will always speak, while the eyes will ever glance towards it. Where do you turn your eyes, your thoughts, and what is inferred from your words? What is the object of your love, your desires? Examine yourself and correct where correction is needed. Finally, often pronounce these words of St. Ignatius: "Conquer thyself." He himself tried, from the moment of his conversion till his end, to conquer himself internally and externally. In this way he became holy. He impressed upon every one whom he tried to lead to a devout life, the maxim "Conquer thyself." He considered this not only useful, but necessary to salvation. And so it is. The world is full of care and misery, because Adam could not overcome himself and refrain from partaking of the forbidden fruit. Hell is full of souls who, because they could not control themselves, went to endless destruction; while heaven is filled with those who practised self-abnegation, and thus worked out their salvation. If you will escape Hell and gain Heaven, conquer yourself; first, wherever this is demanded by a law of God of the Church; and secondly, in things which depend on your own will.

You have daily opportunities for this. Overcome yourself in speaking, hearing and seeing; in eating and drinking; in amusements; in dressing; in working; in praying; in visiting the churches; in confession; in avoiding occasions and persons dangerous to your spiritual welfare. Conquer yourself when your anger is aroused; when you are wronged; when Satan tempts you to sin; when men tempt you. In one word, conquer yourself in all things. How can you do this? Ask your confessor and he will tell you. This is the road in which the saints walked and in which you too must walk if you would enter Heaven. Therefore, let this maxim of St. Ignatius be your constant companion: "Conquer thyself." There is no other way to become holy than to be dead to oneself. Hence, St. Ignatius says further: "Take courage and strive manfully. One heroic act of self-abnegation is more pleasing to the Almighty than many other good works."

Quotes from St. Ignatius

On Detachment:

"God takes special care to detach those whom He loves with special predilection from the passing pleasures of this world, by sending them desires for heavenly bliss, and through the sorrows and bitterness of the present life."

"Before choosing, let us examine well whether the attachment we feel for an object springs solely from the love of God."

Prayer of Detachment by St. Ignatius

Grant, O Lord, that my heart may neither desire nor seek anything but what is necessary for the fulfilment of Thy holy Will. May health or sickness, riches or poverty, honours or contempt, humiliations, leave my soul in that state of perfect detachment to which I desire to attain for Thy greater honour and Thy greater glory. Amen.

On Action and Work

"Let your first rule of action be to trust in God as if success depended entirely on yourself and not on Him: but use all your efforts as if God alone did everything, and yourself nothing."

On Gratitude and Ingratitude:

"In the light of the Divine Goodness, it seems to me, though others may think differently, that ingratitude is the most abominable of sins and that it should be detested in the sight of our Creator and Lord by all of His creatures who are capable of enjoying His divine and everlasting glory. It is a forgetting of the graces, benefits, and blessings received, and as such it is the cause, beginning, and origin of all sins and misfortunes. Contrariwise, the grateful acknowledgement of blessings and gifts received is loved and esteemed both in heaven and on earth."

Physician, Heal Thyself:

"The man who sets about making others better is wasting his time, unless he begins with himself."

"If a man wants to reform the world, either by reason of the authority of his position or the duty of his office, he must begin with himself."

On Abandoning Oneself to God:

"Few souls understand what God would accomplish in them if they were to abandon themselves unreservedly to Him and if they were to allow His grace to mould them accordingly."

Do not Fear, Trust God

"God's love calls us to move beyond fear. We ask God for the courage to abandon ourselves unreservedly, so that we might be moulded by God's grace, even as we cannot see where that path may lead us."

What if Tomorrow Never Comes?

"So you lay your affairs aside till next month or next year? Why, where do you get your confidence that you will live so long?"

How to Act:

"Never say or do anything until you have asked yourself whether it will be pleasing to God, good for yourself, and edifying to your neighbour."

On Suffering:

"If God causes you to suffer much, it is a sign that He has great designs for you, and that He certainly intends to make you a saint. And if you wish to become a great saint, entreat Him yourself to give you much opportunity for suffering; for there is no wood better to kindle the fire of holy love than the wood of the cross, which Christ used for His own great sacrifice of boundless charity. All the pleasures of the world are nothing compared with the sweetness found in the gall and vinegar offered to Jesus Christ. That is, hard and painful things endured for Jesus Christ and with Jesus Christ."

On Love:

"Love ought to manifest itself in deeds rather than in words.... love consists in a mutual sharing of goods, for example, the lover gives and shares with the beloved what he possesses, or something of that which he has or is able to give;

and vice versa, the beloved shares with the lover. Hence, if one has knowledge, he shares it with the one who does not possess it; and so also if one has honours, or riches. Thus, one always gives to the other."

<u>On the Knowledge of God
and Things of this World:</u>

"God freely created us so that we might know, love, and serve Him in this life and be happy with Him forever. God's purpose in creating us is to draw forth from us a response of love and service here on earth, so that we may attain our goal of everlasting happiness with Him in heaven.

All the things in this world are gifts of God, created for us, to be the means by which we can come to know Him better, love Him more surely, and serve Him more faithfully.

As a result, we ought to appreciate and use these gifts of God insofar as they help us toward our goal of loving service and union with God. But insofar as any created things hinder our progress toward our goal, we ought to let them go."

"Beware of condemning any man's action. Consider your neighbour's intention, which is often honest and innocent, even though his act seems bad in outward appearance."

On Virtue:

"Less knowledge, more virtue!"

ജ ❖ ଔ

Some Miracles Attributed to the Holy Water of St. Ignatius

(From "St. Ignatius Holy Water" published by the League of the Sacred Heart, St. Xavier Church,Cincinnati, OH, 1909)

❖   In 1890 Fr. Fiter described three different classes of miracles. 1) In Switzerland the holy water is used effectually against imminent danger from fire, 2) in Spain women experience difficult labours have recorded miraculous interventions through use of the water, 3) in Italy and France it is used as a powerful remedy against violent temptations.

❖ "Thos. D. M,, S.J., was the witness of a ^ remarkable cure of one of the students of Spring Hill College, Mobile, Ala., in 1902. He says that typhoid fever tried them very severely that year.
A young lad named Voorhies, from Louisiana, was attacked. It was a dreadful case, and the doctors gave him up, considering his condition hopeless. His friends began a novena to St. Ignatius, placed a medal of the Saint on the sufferer, and dropped some St. Ignatius Holy Water into all the medicine he took, when lo! the boy was saved. Astonished at the unexpected

cure of their boy, when all natural help seemed useless, the father and mother vowed lasting gratitude to St. Ignatius of Loyola, through whose intercession their son was restored to them."

❖ "O EV. J. B. H., S.J., of the Sacred Heart Church, Sault Ste. Marie, Ont., relates the case of a young man who went to the hospital in the winter of 1903, with a very badly lacerated finger. Blood poisoning had already set in, so that it was in a very bad condition. The surgeon said that there was only one thing to do, and that quickly—amputate it. Sister St. Blaise, who was just then reading the life of St. Ignatius, thought that such a great Saint might find another way, and so she bathed the man's finger in St. Ignatius Holy Water. Shortly after, he went away with four solid fingers and a thumb on each hand."

❖ "About June 4, 1904, Mrs. McC., of Woodward avenue, Sault Ste. Marie, was suffering from tumour. The doctor ordered her to get ready for an operation, if she valued her life. She said she would almost rather die, for she was so broken down that she could not stand the strain. She asked Father B. J. H., S.J., of the Sacred Heart Church, to do something for her. He told her that St. Ignatius would cure her, and gave her some of the holy water. A few days afterwards she was sent to the hospital and lodged in the same room where Sister St. Maurice was cured of the same disease three years before through the intercession of St. Ignatius. The Father reminded her of the fact and gave her his own medal of St. Ignatius to wear during a novena to the Saint. There was no operation. Two months later she told the Father that she did not know how to express her thanks sufficiently to St. Ignatius for the splendid health she enjoyed ever since."

❖ "Father B. C., S.J., writing from St. Ignatius Church, San Francisco, August 31, 1904, mentions a very remarkable case which happened shortly before: A little boy was entirely crippled. His parents having tried in vain all the remedies they could, out in the country where they lived, brought the little boy to San Francisco to consult some of the best physicians. As they first called on one of the Fathers of St. Ignatius Church to learn the name of some prominent physician, he recommended the use of St. Ignatius Holy Water. They started at once to use it, and in a few days the child got so much better that they took him back home to finish the novena. A few days after, the mother sent a letter to the Father, stating that the child was well. Her heart was overflowing with gratitude to St. Ignatius, and she expressed a hope to be able some time to testify her gratitude in a substantial manner."

❖ "August 31, 1904, Father B. C., S.J., of St. Ignatius Church, San Francisco, writes: "About four years ago, as I was going out one day, I met at the door a gentleman who spends much time each day in our church, and I asked him how he was. 'I am not well at all,' he said. 'I have no ambition.' The poor man had intermittent fever and ague, and after walking a few blocks he became exhausted and had to lie down. He took a great amount of quinine, but in vain. I advised him to make a novena to St. Ignatius and to use the holy water. He did not know anything about it, so I explained what it was. He agreed to begin at once. I met him soon after, and asked him how he was. 'First rate. Father,' he said. 'From the moment I took the first dose of that holy water I have been an entirely new man; I never felt better in all my life; St. Ignatius is a great Saint,' etc. I met him again and again since, and he had always the same answer. Before writing to you I saw him again, the other day, and he assured me once more that from the time he took St. Ignatius Holy Water, he has been in the enjoyment of the best of health and that he still feels well. His name is Lawrence K., a member of our solidarity."

❖ "Touring a mission, given in Cincinnati, in the fall of 1905, a wonderful cure was effected through the intercession of St. Ignatius. Mrs. H. H., the mother of a family, had been suffering for two years from an open sore in the leg, which the family doctor declared, after continued treatment, could not be cured. She spoke to one of the missionaries about it, who advised her to apply externally some St. Ignatius Holy Water, and to make a novena. She began the novena, and to the surprise and delight of her family and friends was perfectly cured the third day of the novena. She is now entirely free from any pain, and there is now no longer any trace of the former trouble.”

❖ “The child of Mr. and Mrs. H. E., of Cincinnati, born on Christmas, 1905, was unable to open its eyes for three weeks after its birth, and then was found to be totally blind. The parents consulted the best oculists, but in vain. A friend of the family brought them some St. Ignatius Holy Water, and asked them to apply it to the child’s eyes. They did so. When the friend called again, he was told that the child’s eyes were getting better. Following his advice, they continued to apply the holy water, and within a month, the child could see perfectly. This happened two years ago, and at present writing, January, 1908, its eyesight is perfect, as all their neighbours and friends can testify.”

❖ “Miss C. T., of Hamilton, O., suffered for ten or twelve years from a skin eruption on her face. It was not only very disagreeable in appearance, but was besides extremely painful. She tried several doctors, and used every kind of massage she knew of, but all seemed to afford no relief. In

July, 1906, she began to use St. Ignatius Holy Water. She made a novena, but continued the prayers daily, even after the novena. During the whole time while she and her friends continued the prayers, she applied the holy water several times each day, always hoping she would be cured by the intercession of St. Ignatius. Her confidence and perseverance were amply rewarded, for she was completely cured in a month, and is now (October, 1907) free from all trouble."

❖ "On January 1, 1907, a pupil of the Sisters of Notre Dame, Dayton, Ohio, was cured, by using St. Ignatius Holy Water. The young lady had been ill for three months and the cause of her illness was not known and could not be discovered by her physicians. Her throat became ulcerated and she could not swallow even liquid food. The physicians gave her up and stated that unless she could take nourishment she must die. Her mother, in great sorrow, went to tell one of the Sisters. The Sister at once thought of St. Ignatius and gave her some St. Ignatius Holy Water and a little book that would instruct her how to make the novena. On Christmas day they commenced the novena and on New Year's day, the sick girl asked for some beef tea. It was prepared for her at once and for the first time in nearly four months she swallowed food with ease. Her recovery was rapid. She is now perfectly well. The physicians pronounced the cure supernatural. A beautiful statue of St. Ignatius commemorates the event and testifies to the gratitude of both mother and child."

❖   "A priest in Canada says that he has met cases: (1) in which eczema was cured after bathing the face with the holy water and saying some prayers.   (2) In another case, a child subject to nervous attacks, fits and convulsions was cured. (3) He has found that the sick who use it get rest and peaceful nights. (4) That it is helpful in accident cases. (5) That dying persons seem to receive an increase of faith, and that the priest is greatly aided in administering the Sacraments. (6) There are also many instances on record where women in child-birth have experienced the beneficial effects of this holy water, when used with fervent prayer, and child-like confidence in the intercession of St. Ignatius."

ഇ❖ൻ

Prayer to St. Ignatius of Loyola

O glorious Patriarch, Saint Ignatius, we humbly beseech thee to obtain for us from Almighty God, above all things else, deliverance from sin, which is the greatest of evils, and next, from those scourges wherewith the Lord chastises the sins of His people. May thine example enkindle in our hearts an effectual desire to employ ourselves continually in labouring for the greater glory of God and the good of our fellow men; obtain for us, likewise, from the loving Heart of Jesus our Lord, that grace which is the crown of all graces, that is to say, the grace of final perseverance and everlasting happiness. Amen.

(Indulgence of 300 days)

PRIMA IESU
SOCIETAS
IN
NOVUM
TESTA-
MENTUM
IHS

Illustration Credits

Page 26. *St. Ignatius Loyola*, by Rubens, (1577-1640). Frick Digital Collections.

Page 32. *St. Ignatius Loyola*, photo by 'edenpictures'. Openverse site, licensed under CC BY 2.0

Page 39. *St. Ignatius of Loyola in the Cave at Manresa*, Juan deValdés Leal, (1660). Frick Digital Collections.

Page 44. *Portrait of St. Ignatius*. Engraving, printmaker, Giovanni Marco Pitteri, (1712 – 1786). Rijksmuseum.

Page 52. *St. Ignatius Loyola with an Angel*, Vicente López, (1772-1850). Frick Digital Collections.

Page 59. *Saint Ignatius of Loyola*. Engraving by C. Klauber. (Wellcome). Openverse site, licensed under CC BY 4.0.

Page 62. *The Miracles of Saint Ignatius of Loyola*, Circle of Peter Paul Rubens, (Flemish, 1577-1640). Artvee.

Page 68. *The Madonna and Child with Saints Ignatius of Loyola, Francis Xavier, Cosmas and Damian*, (1629). Artvee.

Page 71. *Saint Francis Xavier and Saint Ignatius of Loyola*, engraving (c. 1633–59), by Schelte Adams à Bolswert after Peter Paul Rubens. Metropolitan Museum.

Page 86. *Saint Ignatius Loyola*, Miguel Cabrera (1695–1768). Artvee.

Page 94. *Saint Ignatius of Loyola and Allegories of the Four Continents (1715–60)*, Felix Anton Scheffler. Artvee.

Page 101. *A family tree of the provinces and colleges of the Jesuit order, with horological markings to show the time in each location relative to noon in Rome.* Engraving after A. Kircher, (1646). Wellcome Collection.

Page 104. St Ignatius Loyola wearing leg splints, by De Favray. Wellcome Collection, licensed under 4.0 International (CC BY 4.0).

Page 107. *The Conversion of Saint Ignatius Loyola*, Miguel Cabrera (1695–1768). Artvee.

Page 110. *Ignatius bezoekt het Heilige Land*, engraving by Theodoor Galle, after Juan de Mesa, (1610). Rijksmuseum.

Page 112. *Ignatius in Spanje*, engraving by Adriaen Collaert, after Juan de Mesa, (1610). Rijksmuseum.

Page 114. *Saint Ignatius of Loyola's Vision of Christ and God the Father at La Storta* (circa 1622), Domenichino (1581-1641). Artvee.

Page 117. *St. Ignatius of Loyola Receiving the Papal Bull*, (C. 1660-1664), by Juan de Valdés Leal, (1622-1690). Frick Digital Collections.

Page 122. Saint Ignatius of Loyola Preaching, (c. 1761), Johann Wolfgang Baumgartner. Metropolitan Museum.

Page 130. *Ignatius of Loyola kneeling before Christ, the Virgin and St Peter*, by Jan Wierix, (Hieronymous Wierix) (1549-c. 1620). Art Institute of Chicago.

Page 139. *H. Ignatius van Loyola*, engraving by print maker: Cornelis Schut (I), (c. 1618 – 1655). Rijksmuseum.

Page 145. *H. Ignatius van Loyola in extase*, engraving by printmaker (after own design), Claude Mellan (mentioned on object). (Date 1608 - 1688 and/or in or after 1676 – 1688.) Rijksmuseum.

Page 153. *Saint Ignatius of Loyola, praying towards the left with a crucifix, a rosary, a book, and a skull on the table in front of him.* Artist and publisher: Lucas Vorsterman I (1595–1675) after Peter Paul Rubens. Metropolitan Museum.

Page 155. *Thesis-Sheet showing Saint Ignatius of Loyola,* (November 15, 1696). Christoph Elias Heiss (1660-1731) after Johann Andreas Wolf (1652-1715). Art Institute of Chicago.

FINIS

Other Books by
Fr. Marin de Boylesve:

A Thought for
Each Day of the Year

ISBN: 978-9893319956

The Blessed Virgin
According to the Gospels

ISBN: 978-9895372607

Little Month of Saint Joseph

ISBN: 978-9899684485

The First and Second Joseph

ISBN: 978-989-53726-2-1

The Sacred Heart of Jesus

ISBN: 978-9893328071

The Month of the Precious Blood

ISBN: 978-9893328088

The Month of Saint Michael

ISBN: 978-9899684492

The Month of Saint Teresa

ISBN: 978-9895372614

Month of Mary – Queen of France

ISBN: 978-989-53726-3-8

Other books by E.A. Bucchianeri
by Subject

<u>Prophetic Visions:</u>

* We Are Warned: The Prophecies
of Marie-Julie Jahenny (E-book)

* Marie-Julie of the Crucifix:
Stigmatist and Prophet (E-book)

<u>The Faustian Legend:</u>

* Faust: My Soul be Damned for the World, 2 Vols.

<u>Lord of the Rings:</u>

- Lord of the Rings: Apocalyptic Prophecies
(E-Book)

Classical Music:

* Handel's Path to Covent Garden

* A Compendium of Essays:
Purcell, Hogarth and Handel, Beethoven, Liszt,
Debussy and Andrew Lloyd Webber

Fiction Novels:

* Brushstrokes of a Gadfly

* Vocation of a Gadfly

Phantom of the Opera:

* Phantom Phantasia: Poetry for the
Phantom of the Opera Phan